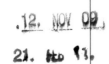
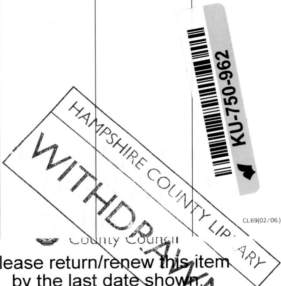

Griffin Publishing Group

ISBN 1-58000-085-1

10 9 8 7 6 5 4 3 2 1

Editorial Statement
In the interest of brevity, the Editors have chosen to use the standard English form of address. Please be advised that this usage is not meant to suggest a restriction to, nor an endorsement of, any individual or group of individuals, either by age, gender, or athletic ability. The Editors certainly acknowledge that boys and girls, men and women, of every age and physical condition are actively involved in sports, and we encourage everyone to enjoy the sports of his or her choice.

Griffin Publishing Group
2908 Oregon Court, Suite I-5
Torrance, CA 90503
Tel: (310)381-0485 Fax: (310)381-0499

ACKNOWLEDGMENTS

PUBLISHER	Griffin Publishing Group
DIR. / OPERATIONS	Robin L. Howland
PROJECT MANAGER	Bryan K. Howland
WRITER	Jason Levin
BOOK DESIGN	m2design group
CONSULTING EDITOR	Chuck Menke

USA HOCKEY

PRESIDENT	Walter L. Bush, Jr.
EXECUTIVE DIRECTOR	Doug Palazzari
CONTRIBUTORS	Heather Ahearn, Dan David
ASSISTANT EDITORS	Art Berglund, Jim Johannson, Matt Leaf, Kevin McLaughlin, Mark Tabrum, Lou Vairo

PHOTOS	ALLSPORT
COVER DESIGN	m2design group
COVER PHOTO	Brian Bahr/ALLSPORT
ATHLETE ON COVER	Brian Leetch

THE UNITED STATES OLYMPIC COMMITTEE

The U.S. Olympic Committee (USOC) is the custodian of the U.S. Olympic Movement and is dedicated to providing opportunities for American athletes of all ages.

The USOC, a streamlined organization of member organizations, is the moving force for support of sports in the United States that are on the program of the Olympic and/or Pan American Games, or those wishing to be included.

The USOC has been recognized by the International Olympic Committee since 1894 as the sole agency in the United States whose mission involves training, entering, and underwriting the full expenses for the United States teams in the Olympic and Pan American Games. The USOC also supports the bid of U.S. cities to host the winter and summer Olympic Games, or the winter and summer Pan American Games, and after reviewing all the candidates, votes on and may endorse one city per event as the U.S. bid city. The USOC also approves the U.S. trial sites for the Olympic and Pan American Games team selections.

WELCOME TO THE OLYMPIC SPORTS SERIES

We feel this unique series will encourage parents, athletes of all ages, and novices who are thinking about a sport for the first time to get involved with the challenging and rewarding world of Olympic sports.

This series of Olympic sport books covers both summer and winter sports, features Olympic history and basic sports fundamentals, and encourages family involvement. Each book includes information on how to get started in a particular sport, including equipment and clothing; rules of the game; health and fitness; basic first aid; and guidelines for spectators. Of special interest is the information on opportunities for senior citizens, volunteers, and physically challenged athletes. In addition, each book is enhanced by photographs and illustrations and a complete, easy-to-understand glossary.

Because this family-oriented series neither assumes nor requires prior knowledge of a particular sport, it can be enjoyed by all age groups. Regardless of anyone's level of sports knowledge, playing experience, or athletic ability, this official U.S. Olympic Committee Sports Series will encourage understanding and participation in sports and fitness.

The purchase of these books will assist the U.S. Olympic Team. This series supports the Olympic mission and serves importantly to enhance participation in the Olympic and Pan American Games.

United States Olympic Committee

Contents

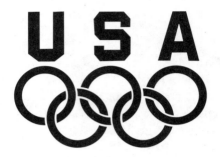

AN ATHLETE'S CREED

The most important thing in the Olympic Games is not to win but to take part, just as the most important thing in life is not the triumph but the struggle. The essential thing is not to have conquered but to have fought well.

These famous words, commonly referred to as the Olympic Creed, were once spoken by Baron Pierre de Coubertin, founder of the modern Olympic Games. Whatever their origins, they aptly describe the theme behind each and every Olympic competition.

Metric Equivalents

Wherever possible, measurements given are those specified by the Olympic rules. Other measurements are given in metric or standard U.S. units, as appropriate. For purposes of comparison, the following rough equivalents may be used.

1 kilometer (km)	= 0.62 mile (mi)	1 mi = 1.61 km
1 meter (m)	= 3.28 feet (ft)	1 ft = 0.305 m
	= 1.09 yards (yd)	1 yd = 0.91 m
1 centimeter (cm)	= 0.39 inch (in)	1 in = 2.54 cm
	= 0.1 hand	1 hand (4 in) = 10.2 cm
1 kilogram (kg)	= 2.2 pounds (lb)	1 lb = 0.45 kg
1 milliliter (ml)	= 0.03 fluid ounce (fl oz)	1 fl oz = 29.573 ml
1 liter	= 0.26 gallons (gal)	1 gal = 3.785 liters

1

Origins of the Game

The exact origin of the game of hockey is unknown, but what is clear is that the sport evolved out of a series of "stick and ball" games played in Northern Europe dating back to medieval days. Northern Europeans who emigrated to North America brought those games with them, and in the middle of the 19th century, several forms of "bandy," "shinty," "hurley," or "hockey" (perhaps originating from the French word *hocquet*, which described a shepherd's crook) were frequently played on ice in both the northeastern United States and in what is now Canada. Some of the players used skates made of bone, wood, or iron, while others wore regular shoes. British soldiers based in colonial cities like Halifax and Montreal were some of the more prominent participants.

In 1862 a new indoor skating facility was built in Montreal. Called the Victoria Rink, it measured 204 feet by 80 feet, nearly the same proportions as the modern hockey arena. The first indoor game played before spectators occurred on March 3, 1875.

The game evolved quickly from that point. The rubber ball originally used was replaced by a block of wood and finally by a hard rubber puck. The number of players on a side dropped from nine to seven, and the concept of a "face-off" was introduced to begin or renew play after a stoppage, giving each team an equal opportunity to gain control of the puck. A Halifax engineer named James George Aylwin Creighton is generally recognized as having created the first accepted set of rules for the new game. Interestingly, during that period, forward passing was not allowed.

Hockey spread quickly, and by the early 1890s there were dozens of teams in eastern Canada, a few in the west, and many more in

Brian Bahr/ALLSPORT

A statue of Lord Stanley at the entrance to Stanley Park in Vancouver, Canada. The inscription reads: "To the use and enjoyment of people of all colors, creeds and customs."

the northeastern United States. From 1888 to 1893 the Governor General of Canada was Lord Stanley of Preston, and he became exposed to the new sport soon after arriving in Ottawa, the nation's capital. Two of his sons joined a local club, and Lord Stanley became an enthusiastic supporter and promoter of the new game. Near the end of his term, Lord Stanley donated a cup to be presented to the "leading hockey club in Canada."

The first team to claim the Stanley Cup was the Montreal Wheelers in 1893. Immediately, the cup became the objective of serious hockey clubs all over the country. Athletes were recruited to play for elite teams in the major cities, thousands of fans turned out for the big matches, and hockey was on its way to widespread popularity.

Hockey was played exclusively by amateurs until early in the 20th century, when professional teams and leagues were formed in Pennsylvania, northern Michigan, and Canada. In 1908 a banker named H. Montague Allan of Montreal donated a cup—still known as the Allan Cup—as an incentive for senior amateur hockey players. By 1912 the professional leagues had spread throughout Canada, producing the game's first star, Fred "Cyclone" Taylor, who, at the time, was earning far more per game than baseball's biggest star of the same era, Ty Cobb.

By 1914 two leagues, the National Hockey Association (NHA)—the forerunner of the National Hockey League (NHL)—and the Pacific Coast Hockey Association (PCHA), had emerged as the strongest in Canada. The Patrick brothers, Lester and Frank, formed the PCHA, which included teams in Vancouver and Seattle, and they were responsible for bringing the concept of "artificial ice" arenas to Canada, which allowed the sport to be played in warmer climates. Artificial ice was created by spraying water on a concrete floor that had been cooled by pumping chilled brine through pipes placed just below the concrete surface. The water would then freeze into a sheet of thin ice.

Through the mid-1920s the two leagues were fierce competitors, with the top team from each league meeting to determine who won the Stanley Cup. In 1926, however, the PCHA folded. As of the 1926–27 season, the NHL consisted of ten teams, divided into the American Division (New York Rangers, Detroit, Chicago, Boston, and Pittsburgh) and the Canadian Division (Toronto, Montreal Canadiens, Montreal Maroons, Ottawa, and New York Americans). The Ottawa Senators were the first champions of this ten-team league, defeating Boston to capture the Stanley Cup. By this time, hockey had become a popular sport throughout Europe and as far away as Australia and Russia. Nevertheless, the northern United States and Canada remained the strongholds of the sport.

The legalization of the forward pass in all three zones of the ice, which came into effect in the late 1920s, made for a much faster-paced, more entertaining brand of hockey, and the popularity of the sport took off. The biggest stars of that era were Howie Morenz, who played most of his career with the Montreal Canadiens, and Eddie Shore, the top defenseman of that time, who spent most of his career as a Boston Bruin.

Another individual responsible for the increasing popularity of the sport was broadcaster Foster Hewitt, whose play-by-play versions of Toronto Maple Leaf games on Saturday nights began airing in 1923 across Canada and in parts of the United States. By 1942 the NHL had shrunk to six teams (Montreal Canadiens, Toronto Maple Leafs, Detroit Red Wings, Boston Bruins, Chicago Black Hawks, and New York Rangers). The league remained that way until 1967, when it doubled in size to 12. At the start of the 2001–02 season, the NHL had 30 teams.

Hockey and the Olympics

With ice hockey as an unofficial sport, the 1920 Olympic Games were held in Antwerp, Belgium, and featured teams from the United States, Canada, Czechoslovakia, and Sweden. The Canadian team, made up mostly of players from the Winnipeg Falcons (who had just won the Canadian championship) dominated play, winning the gold after taking their three games by a combined score of 29–1. The Canadian sweep included a hard-fought 2–0 shutout of the United States, which took the silver after defeating Sweden, 7–0, and Czechoslovakia, 16–0. The teams played seven to a side, there were no substitutions, and the games consisted of two 20-minute periods. If a player was injured, the other team was required to pull one of its players off the ice to even out the sides.

As early as 1908, representatives from France, England, Switzerland, and Belgium had formed the International Ice Hockey Federation (IIHF). Just after the 1920 Olympics, both Canada and the United States joined the IIHF, making the next two Olympic Games the first true IIHF World Championships.

The Canadians, represented this time by the Toronto Granites, won again at Chamonix, France, in 1924, going undefeated in

IOC Olympic Museum/ALLSPORT

Ice hockey competition was conducted outdoors during the
1928 Winter Olympic Games in St. Moritz, Switzerland.

five games and winning by a combined score of 110–3. Again,
the United States took the silver medal, compiling a 4–1 mark,
with the only loss coming against the Canadians in the finals.
Led by Harry Watson, who scored the team's first two goals,
Canada led 2–1 after the first period and went on to a 6–1 win.
Canada won again in 1928 at St. Moritz, Switzerland, in equally
dominating fashion. This time the United States did not send a
team, leaving only Sweden, Switzerland, and Great Britain to
fight it out for the silver (which Sweden won).

With the 1932 Winter Games at Lake Placid, New York, the
United States fielded a team, and once again the Americans
finished second to the Canadians. Due to the worldwide
depression, only four countries (Canada, the United States,
Germany, and Poland) participated in the tournament. The
United States had closed the gap with Canada considerably by
this time. In their two matches with the Canadians, the
Americans lost the first, 2–1, but held Canada to a 2–2 tie in the
second. Had the United States won that second game, a third

and final match would have been required. Instead, after three scoreless overtimes, the second game was declared a draw, and Canada won the gold medal.

Canada's undefeated streak came to an end at the 1936 Games in Garmisch-Partenkirchen, Germany, but it wasn't the United States that finally knocked off the Canadians. Great Britain used a rebound goal by Edgar Benchley to squeak out a 2–1 win over the heavily favored Canadians in the semifinal round. The British team then survived a 0–0 triple-overtime tie with the United States in the final game to win the gold. Canada took the silver and the United States the bronze in what was an eight-team tournament.

There were no Winter Games in 1940 or 1944 because of World War II, but when the Games returned to St. Moritz in 1948, there was a major controversy regarding the participation of the United States team. A year earlier, the IIHF had ruled that the Amateur Athletic Union (AAU) would be replaced as the U.S.

Controversy surrounded the 1948 U.S. Olympic ice hockey team.

governing body for amateur ice hockey by the Amateur Hockey Association of the United States (AHAUS)—today known as USA Hockey. Avery Brundage, chairman of the American Olympic Committee (AOC), accused the AHA of commercial sponsorship and refused to sanction the team. Amazingly, when the time came for the U.S. hockey players to go to the Games, both organizations sent teams. Finally, the Swiss Olympic Organizing Committee decided to side with the IIHF and allowed the AHAUS team to play, forcing the AOC team into the role of frustrated spectators.

After thrashing its first two opponents, Poland and Italy, the AHAUS team dropped a 4–3 decision to Czechoslovakia and was ultimately eliminated from any chance at a medal by a ruling of the International Olympic Committee. The final match featured a battle between Canada and the host country, Switzerland. Because of a disparity in goal totals, the Canadians needed to win by more than two goals to take the gold medal away from the Swiss, and they did just that, scoring a goal in each period and winning by a final score of 3–0.

Canada continued its domination in 1952 at Oslo, Norway, winning the gold yet again, with an overall record of 7–0–1; the only tie came in the final game, against the United States. The American team accepted that outcome, which earned the United States a silver medal, since a loss would have dropped the team to fourth place. The 1952 Games were memorable for another reason—this tournament marked the first time Team USA was penalized repeatedly for rough play. As an example of how heavily the Americans were penalized, three of the U.S. players logged more penalty minutes than any other *team* in the tournament.

At the 1956 Winter Games in Cortina d'Ampezzo, Italy, the Soviet Union entered its first team in the hockey tournament, and the Soviets' clean, crisp style of play overwhelmed the competition, leading to an undefeated record of 7–0–0 and the gold medal. Once again, the United States played the role of bridesmaid, beating out the Canadians for the silver with a 5–2–0 mark.

Canada earned the bronze, but it was clear that the Canadians' 36-year reign as the dominant Olympic hockey country had come to an end.

"Team of Destiny": Squaw Valley, 1960

Having never won a gold medal in hockey at the Olympics, Team USA prepared for the 1960 Games in Squaw Valley, California, as decided underdogs. The Canadians figured to be as strong as always, and the Soviet squad seemed likely to be even better than the 1956 team that had dominated all comers in Cortina. The 1960 U.S. team prepared for the Olympics with an 18-game training tour that resulted in a less than spectacular record of 10–4–4, including losses to Michigan Tech and Denver University.

After two periods of its first match in the Games, Team USA trailed Czechoslovakia, 4–3, and looked to be going nowhere fast. However, the U.S. squad proceeded to score four consecutive goals and went on to a 7–5 win. With their confidence increasing with every goal, the Americans reeled off three straight easy wins over Australia, Sweden, and Germany. Next up was a hotly anticipated game against their longtime tormentors from Canada. Behind a spectacular performance from Jack McCartan in goal, Team USA scratched out a 2–1 win. McCartan stopped 39 of the 40 Canadian shots, including 20 in the second period alone.

Two days later, the "Team of Destiny" met the defending champions from the Soviet Union. Team USA jumped out to an early 1–0 lead when Bill Cleary took a pass from his brother, Bob, and put the puck in the net. The Soviets quickly tied the score, however, and went ahead 2–1 less than ten minutes later. The score remained 2–1 through most of the second period, until Billy Christian took a pass from his brother, Roger, and beat goalie Nikolai Puchkov to tie the score. The score was still tied at 2–2 with less than five minutes to play in the third period when the Christian brothers teamed on the go-ahead goal.

McCartan made the slim 3–2 lead stand up from there, completing one of the biggest upsets in Olympic hockey history. All that remained between Team USA and its first gold medal was a rematch with the Czechs, scheduled for the following morning. The groggy U.S. squad trailed 4–3 after two periods, just as it had in the first game against the Czechs. It was at that point that Soviet team captain Nikolai Sologubov entered the Team USA locker room and, in an act of sportsmanship that epitomizes the spirit of the Olympic Games, suggested that the members of Team USA use oxygen to replenish themselves before taking the ice for the final period. They took his advice, and the result was six consecutive goals for Team USA, led by the Cleary and Christian brothers. The final score was 9–4 in favor of the home team, thrilling the huge crowd and giving Team USA its first-ever Olympic hockey gold.

The Soviet juggernaut rolled to gold at Innsbruck, Austria, in 1964, Grenoble, France, in 1968, and Sapporo, Japan, in 1972, while the best Team USA could muster was a surprising silver in Sapporo. The 1972 Games were notably marred by the absence of a team from Canada. The Canadians had withdrawn from international amateur competition in 1969 because they objected to facing state-subsidized "professional" amateurs from the Soviet Union and other Communist countries. Sweden joined that boycott for the 1976 Games, but by 1980, both had returned to Olympic action. The Soviet team, led by goalie Vladislav Tretiak, continued its hockey dominance at Innsbruck in 1976, going undefeated in five games. Czechoslovakia took the silver and West Germany the bronze, while Team USA finished fifth after compiling a disappointing 2–3 record.

"Miracle on Ice": Lake Placid, 1980

Nobody expected much from the 1980 version of Team USA, which was seeded seventh in a 12-team field. Hockey gold at Lake Placid was expected to go to the powerful team from the

Soviet Union. While Team USA coach Herb Brooks, who was the last man cut from the 1960 Squaw Valley team, was known as an optimist, even he admitted prior to the Games that "I thought we had a chance to go as high as fourth." The 12 teams were separated into two divisions, Red and Blue, with Team USA placed in the Blue division, alongside powerhouses Sweden, Czechoslovakia, and West Germany.

Team USA's first game was against Sweden. Trailing 1–0 with less than a minute remaining, Team USA pulled goalie Jim Craig in favor of an extra skater. Brooks's gamble paid off, as with only 27 seconds left on the clock, defenseman Bill Baker drilled a 55–foot shot that tied the score. That thrilling finish set the stage for one of the great stories in Olympic history.

Next up was Czechoslovakia, which had trounced Norway by a score of 11–0 in its first game. Coach Brooks's young, hungry squad jumped out to an early lead and never looked back, upsetting the favored Czechs, 7–3. Team USA followed that win

Tony Duffy/ALLSPORT

U.S. and Soviet skaters battle along the boards in the semifinal game of the 1980 Winter Olympics at Lake Placid.

Steve Powell/ALLSPORT

Neal Broten of Team USA collides with a Finnish player
during the gold medal match in the 1980 Olympic Winter Games.

with three more victories, over West Germany, Norway, and
Romania, advancing easily to the medal round, in which the
Americans were scheduled to face the defending champions from
the Soviet Union. The two had met a few days before the Games
in an exhibition, and the Soviets had blown out Team USA, 10–
3. The U.S. team that skated onto the ice in the medal round,
however, was playing at a much higher level; the Americans'
confidence was bolstered by the strong five-game winning streak
they'd put together, as well as by a massive crowd that cheered
their every move.

Steve Powell/ALLSPORT

Team USA hockey players hug and celebrate on the ice
after defeating Finland to win the gold medal game of the
1980 Winter Olympics in Lake Placid, New York.

Their energy at an all-time high, Team USA skated on even terms
with the Soviets through most of the first period, but trailed 2–
1 with only a few seconds remaining. With but one second left
on the clock, forward Mark Johnson knocked a rebound past
Tretiak, evening the score. Incredibly, when the teams came onto
the ice for the second period, Tretiak, considered by most hockey
experts the top goalie in the world, had been replaced in favor of
backup Vladimir Myshkin. Down 3–2 early in the third, Johnson
scored again to tie the game, and the crowd, waving American
flags, chanted "U.S.A., U.S.A., U.S.A." Less than two minutes
later, team captain Mike Eruzione took a pass from forward Mark
Pavelich and whistled a 20-footer past a screened Myshkin to
give Team USA the lead. The Russians responded with a flurry
of shots on goalie Jim Craig, buzzing his net repeatedly, but Craig,
who stopped 39 shots for the game, denied everything they threw
at him. As the final seconds ticked off and it was clear Team USA
had sprung the upset, announcer Al Michaels asked the TV
audience, "Do you believe in miracles?!"

While the fans inside the arena cheered and chanted, and thousands more jammed the streets of Lake Placid celebrating, Team USA tried to focus on the task at hand, which was the final game, against Finland. A loss meant the bronze medal, and after two periods Team USA trailed by 2–1. The third period saw Team USA play a passionate, almost flawless brand of hockey. Inspired by an assist on the tying goal from forward Dave Christian (whose father and uncle had led the 1960 team to its upset gold) and sustained by Craig, who stonewalled the Finns at every turn, Team USA scored three unanswered goals to surge to a 4–2 win, capping off the monumental upset and winning the gold medal.

From 1984 Through 1998

The Soviet Union reasserted its international dominance in 1984, going undefeated (7–0) at Sarajevo, Yugoslavia. The Soviets took the gold again at Calgary, Alberta, in 1988, with a record of 7–1. Team USA finished seventh in both Games.

Rick Stewart/ALLSPORT

Ray LeBlanc of the United States saves a shot during a match against Germany at the 1992 Winter Olympics held in Alberville.

Al Bello/ALLSPORT

Hockey's greatest star, Wayne Gretzky, skated for Canada in the 1998
Olympic Winter Games at Nagano, Japan.

The collapse of Communism meant there would be a dramatic
shift in the power base of Olympic hockey at the 1992 Games in
Albertville, France. The state system that had led to the
dominance of the Soviet teams since they entered the Games in
1956 was disintegrating, and the rest of the world was catching
up. The "Unified" team, reflecting the new independence of
nations in the former Soviet sphere, defeated Canada by a score
of 3–1 to take the gold medal, but it was to be the final moment
of glory for the Soviet hockey program that had compiled such
a remarkable Olympic record. The 1994 Games in Lillehammer,
Norway, marked a triumph for Scandinavia, as Sweden captured
its first hockey gold medal in Olympic history, defeating Canada

in the final. Finland took the bronze.

The next major change in Olympic hockey came prior to the 1998 Games in Nagano, Japan, when it was ruled that the NHL would temporarily suspend its season. This meant that the NHL players, all professionals, would be allowed to compete for their native countries, and that the world's best players would finally be competing on Olympic ice. Hockey's greatest player, Wayne Gretzky, was among the NHL players who chose to participate, as a member of the Canadian team.

In the quarterfinal round, Czech goalie Dominik Hasek shut out Team USA, eliminating the Americans. Hasek then blanked Gretzky and his Canadian teammates until the final minute, when Trevor Linden scored to tie the game at 1–1. Forced into a five-player shootout, Hasek incredibly stopped all five Canadian attempts, and when Robert Reichel beat goalie Patrick Roy on the final penalty shot, the Czechs moved on, leaving Canada with only a chance at the bronze, which was lost to Finland. In the final game, Hasek once again proved unbeatable, shutting out the powerful Russian squad, 1–0, and leading the Czech Republic to the gold medal in the first-ever "professional" Olympic hockey tournament.

Women's Hockey and the Olympics

Women's hockey really began in the 1890s, when Isobel Stanley, daughter of Lord Stanley, took up the game. The first league formed in Quebec in 1900 (women hockey players wore long woolen skirts while playing). The next major period of growth for women's hockey in Canada took place after World War I. In the United States the women's game grew much more slowly, and ice hockey didn't really gain popularity among women until the 1960s. Due in large part to the efforts of USA Hockey President, Walter L. Bush, Jr., women's hockey officially came of age in 1990, with the first ever Women's World Championships, won by Canada, which defeated the United States in the final. Canada won the next three world titles as well.

One of the best known female hockey players of that period was Manon Rhéaume. The starting goalie for the Canadian women's team, Rhéaume was invited to training camp with the NHL's Tampa Bay Lightning in 1993 and played briefly in an exhibition game. She went on to play against men in Tampa's minor league organization, holding her own quite well given her relative lack of experience.

Women's hockey became an Olympic sport in the 1998 Games at Nagano, and once again, Team USA and Canada waged a memorable battle for the gold medal. The two met early in the tournament, and although both had already secured places in the medal round, the archrivals battled with tremendous intensity. Canada jumped out to an early 4–1 lead, all on power-play goals, but Team USA responded with six unanswered goals in the final 13 minutes, securing bragging rights along with the 7–4 victory.

Led by forward Cammi Granato and goaltenders Sarah Tueting

Jamie Squire /ALLSPORT

Shelley Looney of Team USA scores past Manon Rhéaume of Canada during the 1998 Olympic Winter Games in Nagano, Japan.

Al Bello/ALLSPORT

Cammi Granato captained the U.S. women's hockey team in 1998.

and Sara DeCosta, Team USA faced Canada again in the gold medal game. Nursing a slim 2–1 lead late in the game, Sandra Whyte flipped in a 40-foot empty-net goal to seal the victory in the final few seconds, setting off a raucous celebration on the ice. Team USA had accomplished its goal of winning the gold in the first-ever Women's Olympic hockey tournament, setting a high standard for the future.

2

Stars of Today
Members of the U.S. Men's Olympic Team, 2002

TONY AMONTE

NHL Team:	Chicago Blackhawks
Position:	Forward
Height:	6'- 0"
Weight:	200
Birthdate:	August 3, 1970
Hometown:	Hingham, Mass.

Amonte is no stranger to heartbreak. He played on the 1991 Boston University team that lost the NCAA title game to Northern Michigan in triple overtime. He also missed the Rangers' 1994 Stanley Cup run because New York had sent him to Chicago just weeks before the playoffs began.

Amonte began attracting attention at Thayer Academy in the mid-1980s, when he played on a line with Jeremy Roenick. The New York Rangers drafted him with the 68th overall pick in

1988, but he remained at Thayer for a year before accepting a scholarship to Boston University. After two seasons at BU, Amonte joined the Rangers for the 1991 playoffs. Traded to Chicago in 1994, he quickly became a fixture with the Blackhawks and emerged as an NHL All-Star.

Rick Stewart/ALLSPORT

CHRIS CHELIOS

NHL Team: Detroit Red Wings
Position: Defenseman
Height: 6'- 1"
Weight: 190
Birthdate: January 25, 1962
Hometown: Chicago, Ill.

Chelios, the U.S. captain, will be 40 years old when the puck is dropped in Salt Lake City. That makes him the oldest man to play for a U.S. Olympic hockey team. Prior to the Olympic debut of NHL players, most Olympians were in their early 20s or younger. Chelios, for example, was only 22 when he played on his first Olympic team in 1984. Asked if he ever dreamed back then that he would be returning to the Games at age 40, Chelios remarked that most NHL players were retiring well before their 35th birthdays, so being an Olympian at 40 would have been unthinkable. He is one of four Team USA members who will become the first Americans to play ice hockey at three Olympic Games.

Chelios has been a fixture in American hockey for two decades. Drafted 40th overall by Montreal after his final season in a Saskatchewan Tier II league, Chelios went to the University of Wisconsin and promptly won a national championship with the Badgers in 1981-82. After another strong season as a sophomore, Chelios joined the U.S. national team for the 1983-84 pre-Olympic tour. He scored 14 goals and 49 points in 60 pre-Olympic games and was a leader of the group that competed at Sarajevo in 1984. After the Olympics, he jumped to the NHL with the Canadiens. In Montreal he made the All-Rookie team in 1984-85 and won the Stanley Cup in his second full pro season. By the late 1980s, he established himself as one of the best defensemen of his generation, going on to earn three Norris Trophies and four first-team All-Star berths. The future Hall of Famer has played in 10 All-Star Games.

Glenn Cratty/ALLSPORT

CHRIS DRURY

NHL Team:	Colorado Avalanche
Position:	Forward
Height:	5'- 10"
Weight:	185
Birthdate:	August 20, 1976
Hometown:	Trumbull, Conn.

Although Drury is a huge part of Boston University hockey history, BU was not the college he had hoped to attend. Eager to follow the lead of his brother and fellow NHL player Ted, Chris applied to Harvard but was not accepted. The Crimson's loss was the Terriers' gain, because Drury went on to rewrite the Boston University record books. His BU teams also won four straight Beanpot Tournaments, including a 2-1 overtime win against Harvard in his senior year. The BU grad is also the only player in hockey history to win both the Hobey Baker Award as college hockey's top player and the Calder Trophy as the NHL's Rookie of the Year—a feat he achieved in back-to-back seasons.

Drury has wasted little time establishing himself as a major force in hockey. Although he emerged on the national sports scene as a pitcher for Trumbull's 1989 Little League World Series champions, he quickly turned his focus to hockey, following in his brother Ted's footsteps at Fairfield Prep. After scoring 37 goals and 55 points in 24 games as a senior, he was drafted by the former Quebec Nordiques with the 72nd pick in 1994. He went to Boston University, where he became the Terriers' all-time leading goal scorer, won the NCAA championship as a freshman, twice earned All-America honors, and claimed the Hobey Baker Memorial Award. He graduated straight to the NHL with the Avalanche (who had relocated from Quebec in 1995). He went on to win the Calder Trophy as the NHL's Rookie of the Year for 1998-99 and played on the Stanley Cup championship team in 2001.

Elsa/ALLSPORT

MIKE DUNHAM

NHL Team: Nashville Predators
Position: Goalie
Height: 6'- 3"
Weight: 200
Birthdate: June 1, 1972
Birthplace: Johnson City, N.Y.

Dunham, the first goaltender named to Team USA for the 2002 Salt Lake City Olympics, also becomes the first netminder to appear on the rosters of three U.S. Olympic teams. Although he didn't play in the 1992 Games, Dunham made the trip to Albertville, France, as a backup netminder. His 1994 performance at Lillehammer, Norway, tied him with Pat Rupp as the only goalies on two Olympic teams. Rupp, a Detroit native who played one NHL game for his hometown Red Wings, was on the Olympic roster in both 1964 and 1968.

Once hailed as the best U.S. goaltending prospect since Mike Richter, Dunham starred at Canterbury Prep as a senior and was drafted 53rd overall by the Devils in 1990. He went the college route, playing three years at the University of Maine. Despite missing most of his sophomore season while touring with the 1992 U.S. Olympic team, he came back to help the Black Bears win the 1993 NCAA title. An All-American in 1992-93, Dunham went to his second Olympics before turning pro with the Devils in 1994. An outstanding minor-league goalie, he saw limited action in New Jersey before being taken first overall by Nashville in the 1998 NHL Expansion Draft. Given the chance to play full-time, he emerged as a star with the Predators.

Robert Laberge/ALLSPORT

BILL GUERIN

NHL Team: Boston Bruins
Position: Forward
Height: 6'- 2"
Weight: 210
Birthdate: November 9, 1970
Hometown: Wilbraham, Mass.

Guerin is the only player on the 2002 U.S. Olympic team who was cut from a previous Olympic squad. It happened in 1992, when Guerin was part of Team USA's pre-Olympic tour. Only 21 at the time, Guerin scored 12 goals and 27 points in 46 games, but missed out on his chance to go to Albertville, France, and play on the team that finished fourth. Guerin, one of the two youngest players along with Keith Tkachuk, was the last forward cut from the team. Six years later he made it to Nagano, Japan, and he was chosen to make his second Olympic appearance a full decade after his tough break in 1992.

Guerin became a hit with scouts and recruiters in 1988-89, when he scored 32 goals and 67 points in the last of his four seasons with Springfield of the New England Junior Hockey League. That led to his making the 1989 U.S. World Junior Team and being the first American selected at the 1989 NHL Entry Draft, taken fifth overall by New Jersey. He accepted a hockey scholarship to Boston College, where he spent the next two seasons before joining Team USA for the 1991-92 pre-Olympic tour. Guerin turned pro with the Devils in 1992, playing five regular-season games and six postseason games. He became an NHL regular the following year. Traded to Edmonton in 1998, he spent nearly three years with the Oilers, but finally came home to Boston in a Nov. 15, 2000, deal for Anson Carter.

Brian Bahr/ALLSPORT

BRETT HULL

NHL Team: Detroit Red Wings
Position: Forward
Height: 5'- 10"
Weight: 203
Birthdate: August 9, 1964
Hometown: Belleville, Ont.

Hull has stirred up a lot of controversy in Canada with his decision to represent the United States in international play. Many Canadians argue that Hull should have followed in the footsteps of his father, who wore the Canadian uniform in the 1972 Summit Series against the Soviet Union. Hull, however, does not consider himself to be Canadian, despite having been born in Ontario. His mother is American, and he was a dual U.S.-Canadian citizen up until 1986, when he opted for American citizenship alone. That was the year that Team USA coach Dave Peterson offered Hull a spot on the U.S. national team that competed at the World Championships in Moscow. Canadian coach Dave King had not been willing to make such an offer, and Hull was so honored by Peterson's gesture that he pledged his allegiance to USA Hockey and has played for U.S. teams ever since.

Born in Canada, Hull is the son of hockey legend Bobby Hull. He spent his first six years in Chicago, where his father was an NHL superstar with the Black Hawks. After moving to the Vancouver area, Brett set his sights on U.S. college hockey and retained his NCAA eligibility by playing with the Penticton Knights of the British Columbia Tier II league. He led that league with 105 goals and 188 points in 1983-84, earning a scholarship to the University of Minnesota-Duluth. Following two stellar seasons with the Bulldogs, including a 52-goal effort in 1985-86, Hull turned pro with Calgary. Just as he was coming into his own, the Flames traded him to St. Louis, at the end of the 1987-88 season. There he would go on to rewrite NHL history, breaking the 70-goal mark in three consecutive seasons and winning the

MVP award in 1990-91. He signed with Dallas as a free agent in 1998 and finally won the Stanley Cup the following season, earning the one honor that had eluded him. Hull, who will join his father in the Hockey Hall of Fame after his retirement, began the latest chapter of his hockey career in 2001 when he signed with Detroit, his fourth NHL team.

Jed Jacobsohn/ALLSPORT

JOHN LeCLAIR

NHL Team: Philadelphia Flyers
Position: Forward
Height: 6'-3"
Weight: 228
Birthdate: July 5, 1969
Hometown: St. Albans, Vt.

LeClair had to make a tough choice following his final season at the University of Vermont. He knew he could delay his professional career and play for the U.S. Olympic team the following year, but the Montreal Canadiens wanted him right away. Although professional players were allowed to play in the 1992 Olympics, the NHL had not yet entered the fray, meaning that LeClair wouldn't be available to the Olympic program that season. Although he therefore missed his chance to go to Albertville, France, LeClair caught a break a few years later when the NHL made his Olympic dreams come true by allowing its stars to take part in the Games.

Few individuals have meant as much to hockey in the state of Vermont as LeClair, who was the first Vermont native to play in the NHL. Born and raised in St. Albans, he attended hometown Bellows Free Academy, where he scored 84 points in 23 games as a senior. Those numbers impressed the Montreal Canadiens, who drafted him 33rd overall, in 1987. Loyal to his state, LeClair opted to play his college hockey with the Catamounts, and earned second-team ECAC honors as a senior at UVM. After his final season, he jumped to the Canadiens and became an NHL regular the following year. He showed his star potential in helping Montreal win the Stanley Cup in 1993, but it wasn't until a 1995 trade to Philadelphia that LeClair came into his own. With the Flyers, he put together three straight 50-goal seasons and became a perennial NHL All-Star.

Rick Stewart/ALLSPORT

BRIAN LEETCH

NHL Team: New York Rangers
Position: Defenseman
Height: 6'- 1"
Weight: 200
Birthdate: March 3, 1968
Hometown: Corpus Christi, Texas

Playing in the Olympics has special meaning for Leetch, who was selected to make his third Olympic appearance at Salt Lake City. That's because Leetch's father, Jack, was cut from the 1960 Olympic team and never had a chance to be part of their historic gold-medal performance at Squaw Valley. He was one of the final players cut, and Brian says his father has never really talked much about that disappointment. Nevertheless, Jack Leetch was truly a star in his own right. He played forward at Boston College and had his best season in 1962-63, when he led BC with 27 goals and earned NCAA East All-America status. His influence has been so strong in Brian's life that Brian and his wife, Mary Beth, named their first child Jack. From his earliest days, Leetch was pegged to be a superstar, and the defenseman made all the prophecies come true.

Although born in Texas, he was raised in Connecticut, where he attended prep school at Avon Old Farms. In two seasons there, he scored a phenomenal 160 points, averaging over three points per game. The New York Rangers drafted him ninth overall in the 1986 NHL Entry Draft, but Brian accepted a scholarship to Boston College, enabling him to retain his amateur status for the 1988 Calgary Olympics. He dominated his lone season at BC, winning Hockey East Player of the Year and Rookie of the Year honors in 1986-87. After touring with the U.S. National Team and playing in the Olympics, Leetch jumped to the NHL and went on to become a two-time Norris Trophy winner and the highest-scoring defenseman in Rangers history.

Brian Bahr/ALLSPORT

MIKE MODANO

NHL Team: Dallas Stars
Position: Forward
Height: 6'-3"
Weight: 205
Birthdate: June 7, 1970
Hometown: Livonia, Mich.

Rarely do NHL scouts agree on a prospect, but in 1988, Mike Modano was a player they all put at the top of their lists. If there was any doubt about his incredible natural talent, he silenced all critics at his first World Junior Championships in 1988, scoring the tournament's most exciting goal, beating a Canadian defenseman one-on-one and then rifling the puck past netminder Jimmy Waite. One scout was so impressed with the move that he told the *Hockey News* that few players at any level of hockey could have scored the goal.

Those who watched Modano play as a youth often say he was the greatest talent they ever saw. With junior teams in Detroit, Modano was clearly head and shoulders above his competition — scoring 131 points in 69 games as a 15-year-old in 1985-86. He made a bold decision at age 16 to go to Saskatchewan and play major junior hockey for Prince Albert of the Western Hockey League, where he continued to dominate and became the top prospect for the 1988 NHL Entry Draft. Taken first overall by Minnesota, Modano joined the North Stars for the 1989-90 season and has never looked back. He moved with the team to Dallas in 1993 and emerged as a 50-goal scorer and the Stars' No. 1 offensive threat.

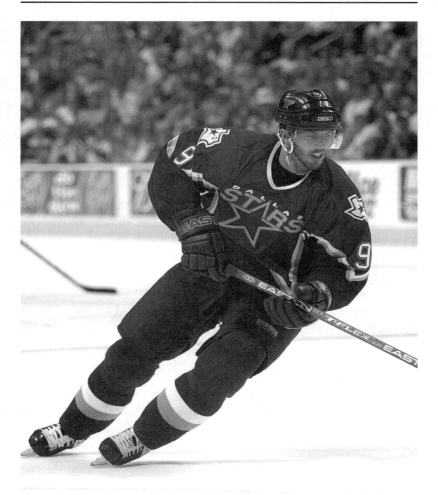

Elsa/ALLSPORT

BRIAN RAFALSKI

NHL team: New Jersey Devils
Position: Defenseman
Height: 5'- 9"
Weight: 200
Birthdate: September 28, 1973
Hometown: Dearborn, Mich.

Given his performance both in Finland and with the Devils, it's still hard to believe that Rafalski is the only member of Team USA who was never drafted by an NHL team. First draft eligible in 1992, Michigan native Rafalski was a veteran of the USHL, NAJHL, and NCAA. He had also played in the World Junior Championships and on the U.S. Select-17 team. A player with his credentials would surely be drafted today, but in 1992, scouts were hung up on size, and he wasn't even ranked among the top 100 prospects. His draft potential was also hurt because he was among the oldest players in his draft class, having just missed the cutoff date in 1991.

Few players have overcome odds to develop into stars like Brian Rafalski. Despite leading Wisconsin to an NCAA title in his senior year, Rafalski couldn't draw interest from NHL scouts because he was considered too small to be an NHL defenseman. So when his collegiate career ended, the Badgers' All-American refused to give up hockey. He went to Europe and played in Scandinavia — something few Americans before him had done. After two years with IF Brynas Gavle of the Swedish league, Rafalski jumped to the Finnish Elite League and instantly became a star. With HIFK Helsinki, he was named the best defenseman in Finland in both 1997-98 and 1998-99. Soon the New Jersey Devils came calling, and as a 26-year-old NHL rookie, Rafalski played a key role for the Devils' 2000 Stanley Cup championship team.

Jamie Squire/ALLSPORT

JEREMY ROENICK

NHL Team: Philadelphia Flyers
Position: Forward
Height: 6'- 0"
Weight: 205
Birthdate: January 17, 1970
Hometown: Boston, Mass.

Spurning college scholarship offers in 1988, Roenick chose to open the 1988-89 season with the Hull Olympiques of the Quebec Major Junior Hockey League. The unorthodox move to Quebec followed in the footsteps of Pat LaFontaine and helped Roenick convince Chicago's front office that he was ready for NHL action just one year out of high school. Roenick utterly dominated the QMJHL with 34 goals and 70 points in 28 games. Despite playing only half the season, he was named to the league's All-Star second team.

As a prep school student at Thayer Academy in Braintree, Mass., Roenick was the dominant force in New England high school hockey. He scored 84 points in 24 games as a senior and was selected by Chicago in the first round of the 1988 NHL Entry Draft. After a brief stint in major junior hockey, he earned him a call-up to the Blackhawks and he became an NHL regular at age 19. In Chicago he emerged as one of the game's top players, stringing together three straight 100-point seasons and scoring 50 goals twice. Traded to Phoenix in 1996, he spent five years with the Coyotes before signing with Philadelphia as an unrestricted free agent in July 2001.

Brian Bahr/ALLSPORT

GARY SUTER

NHL Team: San Jose Sharks
Position: Defenseman
Height: 6'-1"
Weight: 215
Birthdate: June 24, 1964
Hometown: Madison, Wis.

Suter has a very direct tie to the 1980 "Miracle on Ice." His older brother Bob was a member of the team. Gary, then a 15-year-old freshman at Culver Military Academy, was entirely caught up in following the tournament and watching his brother. Seven years older than Gary, Bob was also a defenseman, but he never made it out of the minor leagues during his brief stay in pro hockey. The brothers now have one more thing in common—they can both say they played for coach Herb Brooks at the Olympics.

Suter grew up near the University of Wisconsin campus and was the third of his brothers to play for the Badgers. He prepped for his college career at Culver Military Academy in Indiana and also played with Dubuque of the USHL. He entered the University in 1983 and would carry on his family tradition by starring for the Badgers for two seasons. The Calgary Flames drafted him 180th overall at the end of his fresman season, and after another year of college and a stint with Team USA at the World Championships, Suter decided to turn pro. He wasted no time making an impression in the NHL, winning Rookie of the Year honors in 1985-86 to launch an All-Star career.

Brian Bahr/ALLSPORT

KEITH TKACHUK

NHL Team: St. Louis Blues
Position: Forward
Height: 6'- 2"
Weight: 225
Birthdate: March 28, 1972
Hometown: Melrose, Mass.

Tkachuk was only 19 years old when he played for Team USA at the 1992 Albertville Olympics. That makes him the last teen-ager to have represented the U.S. men's hockey team at an Olympic Games. Prior to 1992, several prominent American teens had played in the Olympics, including Mark Howe in 1972 (age 16) and Al Iafrate (age 17), Ed Olczyk (age 17), and Pat LaFontaine (age 19) in 1984. Tkachuk is also the youngest American player chosen to perform in three Olympics, achieving the feat before his 30th birthday in March 2002.

By the end of Tkachuk's senior year at Malden Catholic, he was considered by most NHL scouts as the top U.S. high school draft prospect despite having missed most of that season with a broken ankle. The Winnipeg Jets picked him 19th overall in the 1990 Entry Draft. He attended Boston University for a year, scoring 40 points in 36 games, before joining Team USA as the youngest player on the 1992 U.S. Olympic team. After the Olympics he quickly established himself as a top Winnipeg scoring threat. In 1996-97 he moved with the team to Phoenix and had his second straight 50-goal season. Traded to St. Louis in March 2001, Tkachuk scored at least 40 goals in four of his first six NHL seasons.

Al Bello/ALLSPORT

DOUG WEIGHT

NHL Team: St. Louis Blues
Position: Forward
Height: 5'- 11"
Weight: 200
Birthdate: January 21, 1971
Hometown: Warren, Mich.

Weight prepared himself for pro hockey as a college hockey star at Lake Superior State University in his native Michigan, scoring 144 points in 88 collegiate games. He was one of the greatest players in Lake Superior State history, but he missed out on winning one of the Lakers' three national championships. His 1990-91 team was considered a lock to reach the NCAA championship game, holding the No. 1 seed in the West. Unfortunately, the Lakers were stunned on home ice by Clarkson in the best-of-three quarterfinal round, losing the final game 4-3. Weight left school after that season, but had he waited one more year he would have more than made up for his disappointment because LSSU came back to claim the national title in 1992.

The former NAHL player was also outstanding at the 1991 World Junior Championships. Drafted 34th overall by the New York Rangers after his college freshman year, Weight joined the Rangers at the end of his sophomore season. New York eventually traded him to Edmonton, where he emerged as a consistent 20-goal scorer and one of the game's great passing artists. He is one of the few U.S.-born players to score 100 points in an NHL season, having tallied 104 in 1995-96. After eight seasons in Edmonton, Weight was traded to the St. Louis Blues on July 1, 2001.

Brian Bahr/ALLSPORT

SCOTT YOUNG

NHL Team:	St. Louis Blues
Position:	Forward
Height:	6'-1"
Weight:	187
Birthdate:	October 1, 1967
Hometown:	Clinton, Mass.

Young is one of only 14 Americans to represent the U.S. at three World Junior Championships tournaments. He made his first trip in 1985, just two months after his 17th birthday, and returned in 1986 to help Team USA win its first World Junior medal, a bronze. Young completed his hat trick in 1987, when he turned in his best international performance with seven goals in seven games. Young saw quite a bit of current USA teammate Brian Leetch during those years, because Leetch also played in the same three tournaments.

Originally a prep school star at St. Mark's in Massachusetts, Young played in his first World Junior Championships as a high school senior. The following year, he accepted a scholarship to Boston University, where he scored 29 points as a freshman. The Hartford Whalers were so impressed that they drafted Young 11th overall in 1986. Young left BU at the end of his sophomore season to join Team USA for its pre-Olympic tour in 1987-88. After the 1988 Calgary Olympics he entered the NHL with Hartford. He played for four NHL teams before finding his current home in St. Louis, where he broke the 40-goal plateau for the first time during the 2000-01 season, his 13th in the NHL.

Elsa/ALLSPORT

Members of the U.S. Women's Olympic Team, 2002

CHRIS BAILEY
Last Team: U.S. National Team
Position: Defenseman
Height: 5'- 6"
Weight: 160
Birthdate: 2/5/72
Hometown: Marietta, N.Y.

OLYMPICS/PRE-OLYMPIC TOUR:
Bailey competed in all six games at the XVIII Olympic Winter Games in Nagano, Japan, recording one assist in the preliminary-round game against Japan ... played in 30 games during the 1997-98 pre-Olympic tour, recording nine assists ... turned in two-assist performances three times—against the ECAC All-Stars, Brown University, and Dartmouth College.

ADDITIONAL USA HOCKEY PLAYING EXPERIENCE:
Bailey competed in 26 of the 39 2000-01 U.S. Women's National Team games, tallying 16 points (7-9) ... appeared in 20 games as a member of the 1999-2000 U.S. Women's Select Team ... contributed four assists ... made her fifth appearance at an IIHF Women's World Championship as a member of the 2001 U.S. Women's National Team (1994, 1997, 1999, 2000, and 2001) ... has recorded 14 points (5-9) in 25 World Championship games ... also appeared on two U.S. Women's Select Teams that competed in the IIHF Pacific Women's Hockey Championship (1995 and 1996) ... named to the All-Tournament Team in 1995 and was selected as the tournament's Outstanding Defensive Player ... appeared on three U.S. Women's Select Teams that competed in the Three Nations Cup (1996, 1998, and 1999) ... notched four assists in 19 career Three Nations Cup games.

LAURIE BAKER

Last Team: U.S. National Team
Position: Forward
Height: 5'- 7"
Weight: 135
Birthdate: 11/6/76
Hometown: Concord, Mass.

OLYMPICS/PRE-OLYMPIC TOUR:
Baker competed in all six games at the XVIII Olympic Winter Games in Nagano, Japan, recording seven points (4-3) ... tallied a goal and three assists against Japan and scored twice in a 7-4 victory against Canada in the preliminary round ... appeared in 30 games during the pre-Olympic tour ... ranked third in scoring with 15 goals and 17 assists for an average of 1.07 points per game ... recorded at least one point in 16 of 30 games and had 10 multiple-point outings, including a hat trick against Dartmouth College and four assists against the ECAC All-Stars.

ADDITIONAL USA HOCKEY PLAYING EXPERIENCE:
Baker played in 10 games for the 1999-2000 U.S. Women's Select Team ... contributed eight points (5-3) ... she made her second appearance on a U.S. Women's National Team at the 2000 IIHF Women's World Championship (1997 and 2000) ... notched four assists in five games in 2000 ... tallied six points (2-4) in five games to finish second among U.S. scorers in 1997 ... named the 1997 USA Hockey Women's Player of the Year for her accomplishments with Team USA and Providence College ... a member of the 1998 U.S. Women's Select Team that finished second at the 1998 Three Nations Cup.

KARYN BYE

Last Team: U.S. National Team
Position: Defenseman
Height: 5'- 8"
Weight: 165
Birthdate: 5/18/71
Hometown: River Falls, Wis.

OLYMPICS/PRE-OLYMPIC TOUR:
Bye competed in all six games at the XVIII Olympic Winter Games and served as the team's assistant captain ... she led the team in goal scoring with five, including two against Sweden ... shared the team's overall scoring lead and tied for third overall among all scorers, notching eight points (5-3) ... recorded at least one goal in four of the six games ... played in 29 games during the 1997-98 pre-Olympic tour ... finished second on the team in scoring with 33 points (21-12) ... turned in 10 multiple-point performances, including a two-goal, two-assist outing against Sweden and a three-goal, one-assist game against the ECAC All-Stars.

ADDITIONAL USA HOCKEY PLAYING EXPERIENCE:
Bye appeared in 34 of the 2000-01 U.S. Women's National Team's 39 games ... contributed 30 points (3-27) ... made her sixth appearance at the IIHF Women's World Championship as a member of the 2001 U.S. Women's National Team (1992, 1994, 1997, 1999, 2000, and 2001) ... tallied seven points (1-6) in 2001 ... finished third overall among all scorers in 2000 with 10 points (8-2) ... tied for second on the team in scoring with eight points (5-3) and tied for first overall in the tournament with five goals in 1999 ... was named a 1999 Second-Team Media All-Star ... has tallied 51 points (27-24) in 30 career World Championship games ... finished second on the 1999-2000 U.S. Women's Select Team in scoring with 31 points (15-16) in 20 games ... appeared on three U.S. Women's Select Teams that competed in the Three Nations Cup (1996, 1998, and 1999) ... honored as the USA Hockey Women's Player of the Year in 1995 and 1998.

JULIE CHU

Last Team: U.S. National Team
Position: Forward
Height: 5'- 8"
Weight: 155
Birthdate: 3/13/82
Hometown: Fairfield, Conn.

USA HOCKEY PLAYING EXPERIENCE:
Chu made her first appearance on a Senior U.S. Women's National or Select Team as a member of the 2000-01 U.S. Women's National Team ... finished the season ranked sixth overall in scoring with 38 points (19-19) in 37 games ... made her first appearance at the IIHF Women's World Championship as a member of the 2001 U.S. Women's National Team ... tied for fourth on the team with eight points (1-7) in five games ... was a member of the 1999 U.S. Women's Select Team that played in the Christmas Cup, Dec. 27-30, 1999 in Füssen, Germany ... among the team's leading scorers with five points (4-1) in four games ... invited to training camp for the 2000 U.S. Women's National Team ... a member of the 1999 and 2000 U.S. Women's Under-22 Select Teams that played a three-game series against Canada in August 1999 and 2000 ... participated in the USA Hockey Women's National Festival (1998-2000).

NATALIE DARWITZ

Last Team: U.S. National Team
Position: Forward
Height: 5'- 2"
Weight: 130
Birthdate: 10/13/83
Hometown: Eagan, Minn.

USA HOCKEY PLAYING EXPERIENCE:
Darwitz notched 35 points (17-18) in 32 games for the 2000-01 U.S. Women's National Team ... made her third appearance on a U.S. Women's National Team at the 2001 IIHF Women's World Championship (1999, 2000, and 2001) ... contributed four points (3-1) ... tallied eight points (2-6) in five games in 2000 ... notched three points (2-1) in five games in 1999 ... both goals came in a 3-1 victory against Finland in the semifinals ... a member of the 1998 U.S. Women's Select Team that placed second at the 1998 Three Nations Cup in Finland ... in 1999 replaced Angela Ruggiero as the youngest player ever (age 15) to be named to a U.S. Women's National Team ... a member of the 1999 and 2000 U.S. Women's Under-22 Select Teams that played a three-game series against Canada in August 1999 and 2000.

SARA DeCOSTA

Last Team: U.S. National Team
Position: Goalie
Height: 5'- 10"
Weight: 130
Birthdate: 5/13/77
Hometown: Warwick, R.I.

OLYMPICS/PRE-OLYMPIC TOUR:
DeCosta appeared in three games at the XVIII Olympic Winter Games in Nagano, Japan, collecting wins in all three preliminary-round games (Sweden, Japan, and Canada) ... compiled an .875 save percentage and a 1.59 goals-against average and posted one shutout (vs. Japan) ... appeared in nine games during the 1997-98 pre-Olympic tour, compiling a 6-2-0 record ... led all goaltenders with a .941 save percentage and a 1.30 goals-against average ... biggest win during the tour was a 3-0 blanking of Canada in the final of the 1997 Three Nations Cup, giving the U.S. its first tournament championship against Canada and marking the first time ever that Canada had been shut out in a game.

ADDITIONAL USA HOCKEY PLAYING EXPERIENCE:
DeCosta posted an 11-1-1 record, including four shutouts, for the 2000-01 U.S. Women's National Team ... recorded a .914 save percentage and a 1.28 goals-against average ... made her second appearance at the IIHF Women's World Championship as a member of the 2001 U.S. Women's National Team (2000 and 2001) ... recorded a 2-0-0 mark with a .500 goals-against average and a .975 save percentage, leading Team USA to its seventh consecutive gold-medal game appearance at the World Championships in 2001 ... a member of the 1998 U.S. Women's Select Team that competed in the 1998 Three Nations Cup ... made her first appearance on a national-level team as a member of the 1996 U.S. Women's Select Team at the 1996 IIHF Pacific Women's Hockey Championship ... also played on the 1995 U.S. Women's National Junior Team.

TRICIA DUNN

Last Team: U.S. National Team
Position: Forward
Height: 5'- 8"
Weight: 150
Birthdate: 4/25/74
Hometown: Derry, N.H.

OLYMPICS/PRE-OLYMPIC TOUR:
Dunn competed in all six games at the XVIII Olympic Winter Games in Nagano, Japan ... scored one goal, the game-winner, in a 7-4 comeback victory against Canada in preliminary-round action ... appeared in 30 games during the 1997-98 pre-Olympic tour and contributed 13 points (6-7).

ADDITIONAL USA HOCKEY PLAYING EXPERIENCE:
Dunn appeared in 29 of the 2000-01 U.S. Women's National Team's 39 games ... missed 10 games due to a broken arm ... notched 21 points (11-10) ... registered 12 points (7-5) in 20 games as a member of the 1999-2000 U.S. Women's Select Team ... made her fourth appearance on a U.S. Women's National Team at the 2001 IIHF Women's World Championship (1997, 1999, 2000, and 2001) ... recorded three assists in 2001 ... contributed seven points (6-1) in five games in 2000 ... notched three points (2-1) in five games in 1999 ... tallied two points (1-1) in five games in 1997 ... appeared on two U.S. Women's Select Teams that competed in the Three Nations Cup (1998 and 1999) ... tallied eight points (1-7) in 18 Three Nations Cup games.

BRANDY FISHER

Last Team: U.S. National Team
Position: Forward
Height: 5'- 5"
Weight: 145
Birthdate: 10/28/75
Hometown: Colton, N.Y.

USA HOCKEY PLAYING EXPERIENCE:
Fisher appeared in 37 games with the 2000-01 U.S. Women's National Team, tallying 32 points (20-12) ... suffered a season-ending knee injury in February ... tied for third among all scorers on the 1999-2000 U.S. Women's Select Team with 26 points (10-16) in 20 games ... she made her second appearance on a U.S. Women's National Team at the 2000 IIHF Women's World Championship (1999 and 2000) ... tied for fourth on the team in scoring in 2000 with eight points (3-5) in five games ... tallied four points (2-2) in five games in 1999 ... appeared on two U.S. Women's Select Teams that competed in the Three Nations Cup (1998 and 1999) ... tallied three points (1-2) in five games in 1999 ... contributed two points (1-1) in four games in 1998 ... one of 54 players at the 1997 USA Hockey Women's Festival, which served as the selection camp for the 1997-98 USA Hockey Women's National Team.

CAMMI GRANATO

Last Team: U.S.National Team
Position: Forward
Height: 5'- 7"
Weight: 140
Birthdate: 3/25/71
Hometown: Downers Grove, Ill.

OLYMPICS/PRE-OLYMPIC TOUR:
Granato competed in all six games at the XVIII Olympic Winter Games and served as the team captain ... tied with three others as the team's scoring leader and tied for third overall with eight points (4-4) ... contributed at least one point in four of the six games, including two-goal performances against China and Canada in the preliminary round ... appeared in 29 games during the 1997-98 pre-Olympic tour and finished as the team's fourth-leading scorer with 31 points (14-17).

ADDITIONAL USA HOCKEY PLAYING EXPERIENCE:
Granato was second overall on the 2000-01 U.S. Women's National Team in scoring, tallying 68 points (36-32) in 38 games ... led the 1999-2000 U.S. Women's Select Team in scoring with 42 points (17-25) in 20 games ... the all-time leading scorer in the history of the U.S. Women's Program with 249 points (129-120) ... she is the only player to have been a member of all seven U.S. Women's National Teams that competed at the IIHF Women's World Championship (1990, 1992, 1994, 1997, 1999, 2000, and 2001) ... is the all-time leading U.S. scorer in the history of the IIHF Women's World Championship with 72 points (43-29) ... led Team USA with 13 points (7-6) in five games in 2001 ... tallied seven points (6-1) in 2000 ... tied for second on the team in scoring in 1999 with eight points (3-5) in five games ... appeared in two IIHF Pacific Women's Hockey Championships as a member of the U.S. Women's Select Team (1995 and 1996) ... a member of three U.S. Women's Select Teams that competed at the Three Nations Cup (1996, 1998, and 1999).

ANNAMARIE HOLMES

Last Team: U.S.National Team
Position: Forward
Height: 5'- 8"
Weight: 150
Birthdate: 5/16/79
Hometown: Apple Valley, Minn.

USA HOCKEY PLAYING EXPERIENCE:
Holmes made her first appearance on a senior U.S. Women's National or Select Team as a member of the 2000-01 U.S. Women's National Team, taking a year off from Princeton University to train with the squad ... contributed 32 points (8-24) in 39 games, seeing action at both defense and forward ... made her first appearance at an IIHF Women's World Championship as a member of the 2001 U.S. Women's National Team ... tallied three points (1-2) in five games ... was a member of the 1999 and 2000 U.S. Women's Under-22 Select Teams that played a three-game series against Canada in August of both 1999 and 2000 ... invited to training camp for the 2000 U.S. Women's National Team ... participated in USA Hockey Development Camps for four years (1994-97) ... played in the 1999 and 2000 USA Hockey Women's National Festivals ... was a member of the 1995 and 1996 U.S. Women's National Junior Teams.

KATHLEEN KAUTH

Last Team: Brown University
Position: Forward
Height: 5'-8"
Weight: 150
Birthdate: 3/28/79
Hometown: Saratoga Springs, N.Y.

USA HOCKEY PLAYING EXPERIENCE:
Kauth made her first appearance at a USA Hockey Women's National Festival in 2001 ... has also attended USA Hockey Development Camps in Lake Placid.

COLLEGE EXPERIENCE:
Completed her senior season at Brown University in 2000-01 ... led the team in scoring in 2000-01 with a career-high 41 points (16-25) in 29 games ... named a Second Team All-Ivy and Second Team All-ECAC selection in 2001 ... ranked fifth in the Eastern College Athletic Conference and among the top 20 scorers in the nation ... has tallied 108 points (52-56) in her collegiate career ... ranked 12th on Brown's all-time scoring list.

COURTNEY KENNEDY

Last Team: University of Minnesota
Position: Defensemen
Height: 5'- 9"
Weight: 190
Birthdate: 3/29/79
Hometown: Woburn, Mass.

USA HOCKEY EXPERIENCE:
Kennedy made her fourth appearance at a USA Hockey Women's National Festival in 2001 (1998, 1999, 2000, and 2001) ... was also a member of the 1999 and 2000 U.S. Women's Under-22 Select Team that played a three-game series against Canada's Under-22 Team.

COLLEGE EXPERIENCE:
Completed her senior season at the University of Minnesota in 2000-01 ... named a First-Team All-American as well as the Western Collegiate Hockey Association Player of the Year in 2000-01 ... led the Gophers with a +39 plus/minus rating ... led all WCHA defensemen in scoring with 41 points (10-31) in 34 contests ... tallied 143 points (53-90) in 130 career games.

ANDREA KILBOURNE

Last Team: Princeton University
Position: Forward
Height: 5'- 6"
Weight: 175
Birthdate: 4/19/80
Hometown: Saranac Lake, N.Y.

USA HOCKEY EXPERIENCE:
Kilbourne made her fourth appearance at a USA Hockey Women's National Festival in 2001 (1997, 1999, 2000, and 2001) ... was also a member of the 1999 and 2000 U.S. Women's Under-22 Select Team that played a three-game series against Canada's Under-22 Team.

COLLEGE EXPERIENCE:
Completed her junior season at Princeton University in 2000-01 ... led the Tigers in scoring for the third consecutive season with 49 points (22-27) in 29 games ... ranked fifth overall in the Eastern College Athletic Conference in scoring ... notched 44 points (18-26) during the 1999-2000 campaign ... tallied 38 points (18-20) during 1998-99, her freshman season ... garnered All-ECAC and All-Ivy League honors in each of her three seasons at Princeton.

KATIE KING

Last Team: U.S.National Team
Position: Forward
Height: 5'- 9"
Weight: 179
Birthdate: 5/24/75
Hometown: Salem, N.H.

OLYMPICS/PRE-OLYMPIC TOUR:
King competed in all six games at the XVIII Olympic Winter Games in Nagano, Japan ... tied with three others for the team's overall scoring lead and tied for third overall with eight points (4-4) ... scored in five of the six games, including a hat trick against Japan ... led Team USA in scoring at the conclusion of the 1997-98 pre-Olympic tour, recording a team-high 23 goals while contributing 16 assists for 39 points in 31 games ... also led the team in points-per-game average (1.26) ... she was credited with at least a goal or an assist in 22 of 31 games and turned in 11 multiple-point outings ... scored four goals against the ECAC All-Stars and notched two goals and two assists against her alma mater, Brown University ... scored a goal in each of the three final contests of the tour and then extended that streak to eight games with at least one point in the first five games of the Olympics.

ADDITIONAL USA HOCKEY PLAYING EXPERIENCE:
King finished the season third overall on the 2000-01 U.S. Women's National Team with 57 points (29-28) in 39 games ... tied for third among all scorers on the 1999-2000 U.S. Women's Select Team, notching 26 points (12-14) in 20 games ... she made her fourth appearance on a U.S. Women's National Team at the 2001 IIHF Women's World Championship (1997, 1999, 2000, and 2001) ... tied for fourth on the team in 2001 with eight points (7-1) in five games ... tallied seven points (1-6) in five games in 2000 ... scored seven points (4-3) in five games in 1999 ... appeared on two U.S. Women's Select Teams that competed in the Three Nations Cup (1998 and 1999).

SHELLEY LOONEY

Last Team: U.S.National Team
Position: Forward
Height: 5'- 5"
Weight: 140
Birthdate: 1/21/72
Hometown: Brownstown Township, Mich.

OLYMPICS/PRE-OLYMPIC TOUR:
Looney competed in all six games at the XVIII Olympic Winter Games in Nagano, Japan ... recorded five points (4-1) ... scored the game-winning goal in the 3-1 win against Canada that gave the United States the first-ever Olympic gold medal in women's ice hockey ... notched two goals and an assist against Japan in the preliminary round ... missed the first nine games of the 1997-98 pre-Olympic tour with a shoulder injury ... played 19 games and contributed 23 points (9-14) for an average of 1.21 points per game, second on the squad ... best outing was against Brown University when she tallied a hat trick and added one assist.

ADDITIONAL USA HOCKEY PLAYING EXPERIENCE:
Looney appeared in 33 of the 2000-01 U.S. Women's National Team's 39 games ... notched 28 points (13-15) ... appeared in three of the 1999-2000 U.S. Women's Select Team's 20 games, contributing one assist ... she made her sixth appearance at the IIHF Women's World Championship as a member of the 2001 U.S. Women's National Team (1992, 1994, 1997, 1999, 2000, and 2001) ... notched four points (2-2) in 2001 ... scored three points (2-1) in 2000 ... tallied four points (2-2) in five games in 1999 ... recorded 33 points (15-18) in 28 career World Championship games ... garnered an Outstanding Performance Award in 1997 for her six-point (4-2) performance ... has twice appeared on U.S. Women's Select Teams at the IIHF Pacific Women's Hockey Championship (1995 and 1996) ... earned an Outstanding Performance Award in 1996 ... also appeared on two U.S. Women's Select Teams that played in the 1996 and 1998 Three Nations Cups.

SUE MERZ
Last Team: U.S.National Team
Position: Defensemen
Height: 5'- 5"
Weight: 145
Birthdate: 4/10/72
Hometown: Greenwich, Conn.

OLYMPICS/PRE-OLYMPIC TOUR:
Merz competed in all six games at the XVIII Olympic Winter Games in Nagano, Japan ... contributed six points (1-5) ... assisted on the first goal against Canada in the gold-medal game ... also tallied one goal against Sweden ... scored at least one point in four of the six games ... appeared in 30 games during the 1997-98 pre-Olympic tour, scoring 16 points (2-14) ... best offensive showing was a three-assist performance against Brown University ... part of the defensive corps that held opponents to a 1.66 goals-against average.

ADDITIONAL USA HOCKEY PLAYING EXPERIENCE:
Merz tallied 24 points (4-20) in 39 games for the 2000-01 U.S. Women's National Team ... played in seven of the 1999-2000 U.S. Women's Select Team's 20 games, registering five points (2-3) ... she appeared in her sixth IIHF Women's World Championship as a member of the 2001 U.S. Women's National Team (1990, 1992, 1994, 1999, 2000, and 2001) ... tallied two points (1-1) in 2001 ... contributed two assists in three games in 2000 ... named a 1999 First-Team All Star for her six-point (1-5) performance ... recorded 20 points (7-13) in 23 career World Championship games ... a member of two U.S. Women's Select Teams that competed in the IIHF Pacific Women's Championship (1995 and 1996) ... played in two Three Nations Cups as a member of the U.S. Women's Select Team (1996 and 1998) ... notched three points (1-5) in 15 Three Nations Cup games.

A.J. MLECZKO
Last Team: U.S.National Team
Position: Defensemen
Height: 5'- 11"
Weight: 160
Birthdate: 6/14/75
Hometown: Nantucket, Mass.

OLYMPICS/PRE-OLYMPIC TOUR:
Mleczko competed in all six games at the XVIII Olympic Winter Games in Nagano, Japan ... contributed two goals and two assists ... appeared in 29 games during the 1997-98 pre-Olympic tour and was Team USA's sixth leading scorer with 26 points on 13 goals and 13 assists ... contributed at least one point in 16 of 29 games ... best outing was a four-goal, one assist performance against Sweden ... started the tour on a four-game point-scoring streak and ended the tour on a three-game point-scoring streak.

ADDITIONAL USA HOCKEY PLAYING EXPERIENCE:
Mleczko led all defensemen in scoring and finished fourth overall on the 2000-01 U.S. Women's National Team with 47 points (15-32) in 39 games ... scored 16 points (6-10) in 20 games as a member of the 1999-2000 U.S. Women's Select Team as she converted from a forward to a defenseman ... she has appeared on three U.S. Women's National Teams at the IIHF Women's World Championship (1997, 2000, and 2001) ... contributed three points (1-2) in 2001 ... tallied eight points (1-7) in 2000 ... contributed two assists in five games in 1997 ... a member of the U.S. Women's Select Teams that competed in the IIHF Pacific Women's Championship (1995 and 1996) ... tallied eight points (3-5) in 10 career Pacific Women's Championship Games ... appeared on two U.S. Women's Select Teams that competed at the Three Nations Cup (1996 and 1999) ... among Team USA's leading scorers in 1999 with four points (2-2) in five games ... named the 1999 USA Hockey Women's Player of the Year.

TARA MOUNSEY

Last Team: U.S.National Team
Position: Defensemen
Height: 5'- 6"
Weight: 150
Birthdate: 3/12/78
Hometown: Concord, N.H.

OLYMPICS/PRE-OLYMPIC TOUR:
Mounsey competed in all six games at the XVIII Olympic Winter Games in Nagano, Japan ... contributed six points (2-4) and recorded at least one point in five of the six games ... appeared in 27 games during the 1997-98 pre-Olympic tour and was Team USA's fifth leading scorer with 27 points on nine goals and a team-high 18 assists ... contributed at least one point in 16 of 27 games ... best outing was a four-assist performance against Northeastern University.

ADDITIONAL USA HOCKEY PLAYING EXPERIENCE:
Mounsey made her second appearance on a U.S. Women's National Team at the 1999 IIHF Women's World Championship (1997 and 1999) ... missed the 2000 IIHF World Championship with a knee injury ... tallied two points (0-2) in five games in 1999 ... notched five points (2-3) in five games in 1997 ... a member of the U.S. Women's Select Team that captured the silver medal at the 1996 IIHF Pacific Women's Championship ... earned the tournament Outstanding Performance Award.

JENNY POTTER

Last Team: U.S.National Team
Position: Forward
Height: 5'- 4"
Weight: 145
Birthdate: 1/12/79
Hometown: Eagan, Minn.

OLYMPICS/PRE-OLYMPIC TOUR:
Potter competed in all six games at the XVIII Olympic Winter Games in Nagano, Japan ... scored five points (2-3), including one goal and one assist against China ... recorded at least one point in four of six games ... played in 24 games during the 1997-98 pre-Olympic tour and tallied 16 points (7-9) ... had two two-goal performances, against the ECAC All-Stars and Dartmouth College.

ADDITIONAL USA HOCKEY PLAYING EXPERIENCE:
Potter made her third appearance at an IIHF Women's World Championship as a member of the 2001 U.S. Women's National Team (1999, 2000, and 2001) ... finished third on the team in scoring with 10 points (3-7) in 2001 ... contributed three assists while playing defense in 2000 ... led the tournament in 1999 with 12 points (5-7) in five games ... named the tournament's Most Outstanding Forward and was selected to the tournament All-Star Team ... a member of the 1998 U.S. Women's Select Team that placed second at the 1998 Three Nations Cup in Finland.

ANGELA RUGGIERO
Last Team: U.S.National Team
Position: Defensemen
Height: 5'- 9"
Weight: 190
Birthdate: 1/3/80
Hometown: Simi Valley, Calif.

OLYMPICS/PRE-OLYMPIC TOUR:
Ruggiero competed in all six games at the XVIII Olympic Winter Games in Nagano, Japan ... appeared in all but one game (31 of 32) during the 1997-98 pre-Olympic tour, contributing 17 points (5-12) ... put together a five-game point-scoring streak from Oct. 11 through Oct. 25.

ADDITIONAL USA HOCKEY PLAYING EXPERIENCE:
Ruggiero took the year off from Harvard University and finished second among all defenseman and fifth overall with 43 points (15-28) in 39 games for the 2000-01 U.S. Women's National Team ... appeared in two games for the 1999-2000 U.S. Women's Select Team ... she made her fourth appearance at an IIHF Women's World Championship as a member of the 2001 U.S. Women's National Team (1997, 1999, 2000, and 2001) ... was the second highest scoring defensemen on the team in 2001, tallying six points (2-4) in five games ... registered seven points (1-6) in 2000 ... tallied two points (1-1) in 1999 ... contributed one assist in five games in 1997 ... a member of the 1996 U.S. Women's Select Team that captured the silver medal at the 1996 IIHF Pacific Women's Championship ... tallied three points (2-1) in five games.

SARAH TUETING
Last Team: U.S.National Team
Position: Goalie
Height: 5'- 7"
Weight: 140
Birthdate: 4/26/76
Hometown: Winnetka, Ill.

OLYMPICS/PRE-OLYMPIC TOUR:
Tueting appeared in four games at the XVIII Olympic Winter Games in Nagano, Japan ... compiled a 1.15 goals-against average and a .937 save percentage to lead all goaltenders in the competition ... stopped 21 of 22 shots in the gold-medal game against Canada to earn the victory ... played in 13 games during the 1997-98 pre-Olympic tour, posting a 10-2-1 overall record, a 1.47 goals-against average, and a .914 save percentage ... four of her 10 wins on the tour were shutouts.

ADDITIONAL USA HOCKEY PLAYING EXPERIENCE:
Tueting posted a team-leading 14-0-0 record for the 2000-01 U.S. Women's National Team with a .898 save percentage ... also led the team in goals-against average (.814) and shutouts (8) ... appeared in three games for the 1999-2000 U.S. Women's Select Team ... made her third appearance on a U.S. Women's National Team at the 2001 IIHF World Championship (1997, 2000, and 2001) ... turned in a 2-1-0 mark, 1.01 goals-against average, and .933 save percentage in 2001 ... posted a 2-0-0 record, .500 goals-against average, and .944 save percentage in 2000 ... she made her first appearance on an elite-level U.S. women's team as a member of the 1996 U.S. Select Team at the Three Nations Cup in Ottawa, Ontario ... appeared in one game as a member of the 1997 U.S. National Team at the 1997 IIHF Women's World Championship.

NICOLE ULIASZ

Last Team: University of Wisconsin
Position: Defensemen
Height: 5'- 9"
Weight: 160
Birthdate: 7/15/81
Hometown: Perkasie, Pa.

USA HOCKEY PLAYING EXPERIENCE:
Uliasz has made five appearances at USA Hockey Women's National Festivals (1997, 1998, 1999, 2000, and 2001).

COLLEGE EXPERIENCE:
Completed her freshman season at the University of Wisconsin in 2000-01 ... finished ninth on the team in scoring with 18 points (6-12) ... ranked fifth among Western Collegiate Hockey Association rookie defensemen ... also ranked 14th overall among league rookies in scoring ... notched points in four of her first five collegiate games ... ranked among team leaders with a +13 plus/minus rating.

LYNDSAY WALL

Last Team: Syracuse Stars
Position: Defensemen
Height: 5'- 8"
Weight: 142
Birthdate: 5/12/85
Hometown: Churchville, N.Y.

USA HOCKEY PLAYING EXPERIENCE:
Wall made her first appearance at a USA Hockey Women's National Festival in 2001 ... participated in both the 16-17 and 18-19 USA Hockey Women's Development camps in the summer of 2001 ...was the youngest player invited to the 2001 USA Hockey Women's National Festival ... was selected as the youngest member of the 2001-02 USA Hockey Women's National Team.

OTHER RECENT EXPERIENCE:
Led the Syracuse Stars to the 2001 USA Hockey Girls' 19-and-Under National Championship ... notched 65 points (22-43) in 63 games in 2000-01 ... was a member of the Buffalo (N.Y.) Regals Boys' Bantam Minor AAA team during the 1999-2000 season ... captained the Rochester Americans Peewee Major AAA Boys' team in 1998-1999.

KRISSY WENDELL

Last Team: U.S. National Team
Position: Forward
Height: 5'- 6"
Weight: 155
Birthdate: 9/12/81
Hometown: Brooklyn Park, Minn.

USA HOCKEY PLAYING EXPERIENCE:
Wendell tallied 72 points (37-35) in 38 games for the 2000-01 U.S. Women's National Team ... led the squad in points, goals, and assists ... was the team's leading scorer in 15 of the 38 games in which she appeared ... made her third appearance on a U.S. Women's National Team at the 2001 IIHF Women's World Championship (1999, 2000, and 2001) ... among tournament leaders with 12 points (3-9) in 2001 ... led all scorers at the 2000 tournament with 13 points (2-11) in five games ... tied for fifth on the team in scoring with six points (3-3) in five games in 1999 ... honored with the USA Hockey Women's Player of the Year Award at the 2001 USA Hockey Annual Congress and with the Bob Johnson Award for excellence in international competition at the 2000 USA Hockey Annual Congress ... a member of the 1998 U.S. Women's Select Team that placed second at the 1998 Three Nations Cup in Finland ... contributed two points (2-0) in four games ... participated in the 1998 USA Hockey Women's Festival and the 1997 USA Hockey Women's Festival, which served as the selection camp for the 1997-98 USA Hockey Women's National Team.

CARISA ZABAN

Last Team: U.S.National Team
Position: Forward
Height: 5'- 7"
Weight: 135
Birthdate: 9/12/77
Hometown: Glenview, Ill.

USA HOCKEY PLAYING EXPERIENCE:
Zaban made her first appearance on a Senior U.S. Women's National or Select Team as a member of the 2000-01 U.S. Women's National Team ... contributed 19 points (8-11) in 28 games ... made her first appearance at the IIHF Women's World Championship as a member of the 2001 U.S. Women's National Team ... notched four points (3-1) in five games ... played in three USA Hockey Women's National Festivals (1997-99).

COLLEGE EXPERIENCE:
Completed her senior season at the University of New Hampshire in 1999-2000 ... finished third in the nation and first overall in the Eastern College Athletic Conference with 72 points (35-37) in 33 games during the 1999-2000 season ... scored her 256th career point on Feb. 20, 2000, becoming the Wildcats' all-time leading scorer ... one of four finalists for the 2000 Patty Kazmaier Memorial Award, presented annually to the nation's top intercollegiate varsity women's ice hockey player ... led UNH in scoring all four seasons of her career.

3

Getting Started

Ice hockey is a fast-paced game played on a frozen surface by two teams of six players each. All of the players wear skates and carry a wooden stick that curves at the bottom. They use the sticks to propel the playing piece, called the *puck*, across the ice and into a net to score a goal. The object of the game is for one team to score more goals than the other team. Each team tries to retain—or steal—the puck to score a goal against the opposing team.

The principle guiding the rules of hockey is one of continuous action. Each team attempts to play flawlessly so as to avoid penalties and stoppage of the game. Generally, a referee, two linesmen, and several off-ice officials are employed to monitor the action, and only they can stop the game. For example, if a player is having difficulties staying in the play, or wants a rest, or even breaks his or her stick, he or she must deal with these problems while the game continues.

Most of the rules of hockey are simple and logical. They keep the game moving while protecting the players from physical injury. Once you learn the rules, you're well on your way to participating in and enjoying a great sport.

The Rink

Ice hockey is played on a sheet of ice called a *rink*. Many cities have ice rinks, often located inside an arena.

A standard NHL-sized rink is 85 feet wide and 200 feet long, with rounded corners. An Olympic-sized rink is 98.5 feet wide and 197 feet long. The ice is enclosed by plastic or fiberglass walls, known as "the boards," which are designed to protect the fans and prevent the puck from accidentally leaving the arena or flying into the stands. The boards are 42 inches high and are called "sideboards" along the length of the rink and "end boards" behind the goals. Often, rinks have shatterproof glass that rises beyond the boards to further protect spectators.

Embedded in the ice is a sequence of red and blue lines that demarcate various zones. These lines are continued and drawn on the boards as well.

- Two blue lines divide the ice into three sections: the defending zone, the attacking zone, and the neutral zone (between the other two). Each blueline is placed 60 feet from each goal

Simon Bruty/ALLSPORT

An overhead view of goalmouth action

line.

- A red center line divides the ice in half. This line is located in the neutral zone between the two blue lines.

- Two red goal lines are located 13 feet from the end boards, one at each end of the rink.

At the center of each red goal line sits the *goal*. The goal cage consists of a frame and two goal posts joined by a metal crossbar and covered with a net of white nylon cord. The goal is 4 feet high and 6 feet wide. In order for a goal to be scored, the puck must pass through the front of the goal. When that happens, a red light behind the goal is lit by the goal judge.

Drawn on the ice in front of the goal is the *goal crease*, a 6-foot semicircular area. Attacking players may only enter this area if the puck is in it. One player from each team, called the *goalie*, is allowed to remain in the goal crease. The goalie's job is to protect the team's goal, preventing players from the opposing team from scoring.

The neutral zone in the center of the rink is neutral for both teams. One team's defending zone is the other team's attacking zone.

Several other circles are also drawn onto the ice. They are used by the referee or linesmen to put the puck into play and, when necessary, to restart the action by means of a face-off (see Chapter 4, "Ready to Play").

Simon Bruty/ALLSPORT

An overhead view of the face-off

- The blue or red circle in the middle of the rink is the center face-off circle.

- There are four red face-off spots in the neutral zone.

- Two red face-off circles are located at each end of the rink near the goal lines.

Brian Bahr/ALLSPORT

Alexander Khavanov of the St. Louis Blues enters the penalty box
for a double minor high-sticking penalty.

On one side of the rink, behind the sideboards, are the team
benches. While only six players are allowed on the ice at one
time, a National Hockey League team may have a maximum of
20 players (23 for men's Olympic Teams). The coaches, managers,
and trainers also stand behind the team bench.

Penalty boxes are benches where players who have broken a rule
(committed a penalty) are forced to sit until their penalty time is
up. The penalty boxes are usually located across the ice from
the team benches.

The timekeeper and the official scorer also sit on benches behind
the sideboards between the two penalty boxes.

Equipment

Hockey is a sport that requires special equipment: a uniquely padded uniform and helmet, and of course ice skates and a stick. Goalie equipment differs in many ways from that of the other players.

Helmet

Use of a helmet is mandatory in hockey, since injuries that arise from a blow to the head are serious and can even cause a concussion. The helmet is a lightweight, plastic-padded head protector, with holes on the sides for proper ventilation.

Any helmet you choose should fit the shape of your head. It needs to be snug, but not too tight. Expect to pay between $45 and $125 for a helmet with a face protector, which is essential. There are two kinds of face shields: the Lexan plastic see-through models and the wire-cage models. Any face shield needs to provide protection for your jaw and teeth as well as your eyes and nose.

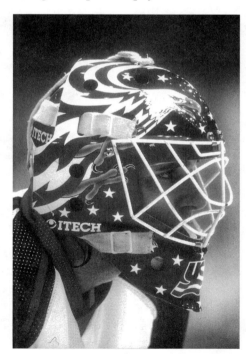

Clive Brunskill/ALLSPORT

The mask of Garth Snow at the 1994 Lillehammer Winter Olympics

Mouth Guard

The mouth guard protects your teeth from breaking, your tongue from being bitten, and your brain from concussion. Expect to pay from $5 for a simple device to

$40 for a custom-fitted mouth guard, a bargain compared to the price of dental work.

Hockey Stick

Hockey players use many different kinds of materials for their L-shaped sticks, which consist of two connected parts: the handle, or shaft, and the blade. Sticks can be made from aluminum, graphite, Kevlar, composites, fiberglass, and, of course, wood. There are s h a f t - a n d - b l a d e combination sticks and one-piece sticks as well. Prices can run from $15 for an inexpensive wooden stick to $175 for the latest professional-quality stick. Advanced players always have at least one replacement

Steve Babineau/ALLSPORT

Calle Johansson of the Washington Capitals fixes his hockey stick.

stick on hand, because hockey sticks can and do break.

Sticks can be a maximum of 63 inches long, measured from the heel (where the shaft and blade meet) to the end of the shaft. The blade must not be more than 12 inches long and 2–3 inches high, and it must have beveled edges. The blade can have a slight curve (up to 1/2 inch) or can angle to the left or the right. Adhesive tape may be wrapped around the stick blade at any place for reinforcement or to improve the stick's handling abilities.

As to the height of the stick, the rule of thumb is that the top of the stick should reach between the bottom of your chin and your nose when you are standing in your skates. For youth hockey, you can lop off the top of the stick to get it to fit correctly.

The Puck

The puck is a vulcanized rubber disk that is 1 inch thick and 3 inches in diameter. It weighs between 5 1/2 and 6 ounces. To reduce the bounce of the rubber and to increase the speed (to over 100 miles per hour), pucks are frozen before professional hockey games and replaced throughout the game.

Skates and Boots

Each hockey player wears special ice hockey skates with very sharp steel blades that are rockered, or curved, at the front and back. Rockered blades make it easier for players to start and turn quickly. In professional hockey, the blades are often sharpened before each game.

To protect the feet, the boots are heavily padded (the padding extends up the ankle). The boots of goalies and defensemen are stronger than those of the forwards, the offensive players, because defenders are more likely to get hit in the feet by shots from the opposing team.

Socks

Socks are divided into two categories. The first type consists of the leggings that players wear above their skates. These are used to keep the shin pads on straight. Each team wears leggings with distinctive colors. This helps players using their peripheral vision to differentiate between their teammates and players on the opposing team.

For foot protection inside the boot, most players prefer a light, thin sock. Layers of socks will hamper performance. Many professional hockey players refuse to wear socks at all, claiming they get a better feel for the ice that way.

Gloves

Gloves, used to protect the hands and arms, can be made from a variety of materials, including nylon, leather, or a combination of the two. Players need to select gloves that fit well and offer a suitable amount of protection to the wrist, thumb, and fingers. The palm area of the glove must be soft enough to allow freedom of movement and a feel for the stick. Make sure you dry out your gloves after you use them, or they will develop an unpleasant odor.

Glove styles can be either long or short. A short-cuffed style will leave your wrist exposed and more prone to getting hit if you don't wear wrist guards. Gloves can run between $50 and $150 per pair, but you can find used gloves for less at hockey exchanges and used equipment stores. The palms of the gloves can be replaced if they wear out, saving the cost of buying a whole new pair.

Pants

Built into the pants are protectors for the thighs, low back, kidneys, and hips. Pants should fit somewhat loosely to allow for a proper range of movement when you skate. Good pants are lightweight and dry quickly. They cost between $80 and $150 per pair.

Jerseys

The jersey or sweater is the outer garment bearing the team logo. Each hockey player has a home jersey and an away jersey. The home jersey is usually white; the away jersey is more colorful. On the front of the jersey is the team emblem, and on the back is the player's number and, often, the player's name. Make sure to wear a jersey that fits right. You have no time during a game to fiddle with a jersey that is too tight or too big.

Padding

Defensemen and forwards wear the same basic protective equipment. Under a loose-fitting jersey and pants they wear a T-shirt, shoulder pads with rib protection attached, elbow pads, and an athletic supporter specifically designed for the roughness of hockey. All players wear padded gloves that protect the hands and wrists, as well as shin pads.

Goalie Equipment

Goalies wear the same basic uniform as their teammates, but they also wear special protective clothing that weighs up to 40 pounds more than the regular uniform. Goalie equipment is both essential and expensive, and can cost between $700 and $1,700.

While goalies are not supposed to be touched in hockey, their special uniform padding is designed to protect them from the onslaught of sticks, pucks, and bodies. There is a difference in the shoulder pads that male and female goalies wear. While most hockey equipment is unisex, the female shoulder pads are adjusted for breast protection, and they extend to the length of the arms.

Instead of the regular shin guards that other ice hockey players wear, a goalie wears pads that are at least 4 inches thick and wrap around the leg from the ankle to the thigh, outside their socks. Goalies also wear this thicker padding on their shoulders, arms, and chests.

Goalie gloves also differ from regular gloves and even differ from each other. The glove on the stick hand is called the "blocker glove" or the "waffle pad," a name that originated in the old days when the glove was a rectangular pad riddled with holes that made it look like a waffle. The blocker glove is used to knock the puck away when it is being shot at the goal. On the goalie's other hand is the "catching glove," which is similar to a modified first baseman's mitt. Catching gloves cost between $85 and $300. A goalie can use a catching glove to scoop up the puck, hold it, and drop it away from the goal.

Goalie skates are also different—they are heavier than normal hockey skates and usually do not have an open space between the skate blade and the bottom of the skate. This prevents the puck from accidentally passing through that space and into the net. They also have molded plastic around the skate to better protect the foot.

Goalie sticks are also wider than the regular playing stick. These special sticks take more abuse (especially from the pucks that sometimes hit at speeds of 100 miles an hour).

Kellie Landis/ALLSPORT

A view of an ice resurfacer machine at work

The Ice Resurfacer Machine

No professional hockey game can start until the ice has been cleaned and smoothed out by the Zamboni® (or Olympia—the other popular brand), a machine named after its inventor, Frank Zamboni. While driven around the rink, the Zamboni® simultaneously shaves off the top layer of ice and sprays a fresh coat of water. The water quickly freezes, making a fresh ice surface to play on. In most cases, the ice is also resurfaced before the start of each period of play.

Learning the Basics

Length of the Game

In pro hockey each game has three 20-minute periods. A large, easily visible clock constantly counts down the minutes and seconds of play, showing the players and fans exactly how much time has passed and how much is left. The clock is stopped when play stops and is restarted when play resumes. There is a 15-minute intermission between periods. Counting timeouts and other stoppages, a game normally takes from two to three hours.

Overtime

In the National Hockey League, if both teams are tied at the end of three 20-minute periods during a regular season game, a five-minute "sudden death" overtime is played. This overtime period follows the end of the third period, after a two-minute intermission. "Sudden death" means the first team to score a goal wins—the game ends even if the time is not completed. If both teams are tied after one overtime, the game ends in a tie. The exception to this rule occurs in postseason playoffs, where there can be no ties. In the NHL playoffs, an unlimited number of overtime periods are played until a winner is decided.

In international and Olympic playoffs, a 10-minute "sudden death" period is played. If neither team scores, the game is decided by penalty shots. Under the rules for a penalty shot, a single offensive player takes the puck from the center ice face-off circle and skates toward the goal, going one-on-one against the opposing goaltender. The team scoring the most goals on penalty shots wins the game.

Timeouts

Hockey teams are allowed only one 30-second timeout per game. Only the referee can stop play—even if a player is seriously injured.

Choosing Sides

The home team starts the game defending the goal closest to its team bench. The teams switch goals during each successive period.

Attacking

"Attacking" is the term for trying to score a goal. When a player "has the puck"—in other words, when his or her stick is touching or moving the puck—and is attempting to score a goal, that player is on the attacking team, or offense. The player with the puck has several options:

- Shoot the puck directly toward the net in an effort to score a goal.

- Pass the puck to a teammate.

- Shoot the puck deep into the opposing team's zone, so a teammate can retrieve the puck and get a good shot on net.

A player is allowed to kick the puck—except in an effort to score a goal. If a player kicks the puck into the net, the goal will be disqualified. Except for the purpose of scoring a goal, kicking the puck is acceptable for a player who has lost or broken a stick.

A player may slap the puck with an open hand, and may catch it and drop it as well. However, a puck cannot be hand-slapped

Elsa/ALLSPORT

Cammi Granato of Team USA takes a shot on Kim St. Pierre of Canada during the 2001 Women's World Hockey Championship.

into the goal, nor can the attacking player use the hands to direct the puck to a teammate.

Shooting

A player shoots when he or she moves the puck toward an opponent's goal in an attempt to score. There are many different types of shots:

- **Wrist shot:** Made with the stick blade kept on the ice. The puck is propelled toward the net by a strong flicking of the wrist. The wrist shot is usually slower but more accurate than a slap shot.

- **Slap shot:** An extremely high-speed shot. The player begins by raising the stick in a backswing, with the stronger hand held low on the shaft and the other hand on the end as a fulcrum As the stick comes down toward the puck, the player leans into the stick to put power behind the shot, adding velocity to the puck. The slap shot is faster and less accurate than the wrist shot.

- **Backhand shot**: Like the wrist shot, but made with a backhand rather than a forehand motion.

- **Flip shot**: The puck is cupped in the stick, which is then flipped with the wrists, lifting the puck off the ice and toward the goal.

- **Snap Shot**: The short version of the slap slot, with the blade drawn 6-8 inches back before shooting.

Brian Bahr/ALLSPORT

Rob Blake of the Colorado Avalanche takes a slap shot.

Passing

A player passes the puck by using the stick to send the puck to a teammate. Passing helps move the puck closer to the goal, keeps the puck away from the opponents, and allows the player who is in the best position the opportunity to score a goal. There are several different kinds of passes:

- **Flat pass**: The puck remains on the surface of the ice.

- **"Saucer" pass**: The puck leaves the ice and flies through the air.

- **Drop pass**: While moving to a new position, the skater leaves the puck on the ice for a teammate to pick up.

Defense

"Defense" is a term that means trying to stop the other team from scoring. The defense, or the defending team, is the team that does not have the puck in its possession. The defending players try to get the puck away from the offensive player who controls it. The five skaters on the defending team try to steal the puck as it is being passed, block the shots headed toward the goal, or take the puck away from a player who has it. The two acceptable methods for stopping an opponent are *checking* and *blocking*.

Checking is bumping into an opponent in possession of the puck by using the stick, shoulders, or hips. Checking is only allowed against the player in control of the puck, or against the last player who controlled it. There are two main types of checks:

ALLSPORT

Scott Stevens of the New Jersey Devils checks Wayne Presley against the boards during a game against the Buffalo Sabres.

• **Stick check:** The defender uses the stick to hook, poke, or sweep the puck away from the attacker.

• **Body check:** The defender uses his or her body to bump or slam into the attacker, employing the hips or shoulders to block the attacker's progress and throw the attacker off balance.

Blocking is less common than checking. In blocking, a player drops to one or both knees and uses his or her body to stop the puck. This is risky because a smart puck carrier can get around a defender who kneels too soon.

If a player uses other illegal methods to gain control of the puck or stop the opponents, the referee will call a penalty (see Chapter 4, "Ready to Play").

Face-offs

A face-off initiates play at the beginning of the game, at the start of each period, and after action has been stopped. In a face-off, an official drops the puck between two opposing players. The players stand one stick length apart, each facing the opponent's end of the ice. The blades of their sticks must be touching the ice, and no other players can be within 15 feet of the players taking part in the face-off. If either of the players in the face-off is out of position when

Simon Bruty/ALLSPORT

U.S. and Finnish team members face off against each other.

the official is ready to drop the puck, the official can ask a teammate of the offending player to be in the face-off instead.

In the face-off, each player tries to direct the puck (after it has been dropped) to a teammate or shoot it toward the opponents' goal. The face-off ensures that both teams have an equal chance of getting to the puck, although some players are better than others at winning face-offs. Except at the beginning of the period, a face-off is usually held at the face-off spot nearest to where play was stopped. There are nine face-off spots on the ice: two in each end, on opposite sides of the goal crease; four in the neutral zone, outside the blue lines; and one at center ice.

Stopping Play

Play may be stopped:

- If a player breaks a rule and is called for a penalty.

- If the goalie stops a shot and holds onto the puck.

- If the puck goes "out of play" or flies out of the rink.

- If the referee ascertains that a player has been seriously injured.

- If the goal cage is dislodged and moved off its proper position.

- If a player is injured and his or her team has possession of the puck.

- If a player catches the puck in his or her hand and the puck is declared "dead."

- If the puck is "frozen" between two players, which means the puck is caught between the sticks and/or skates of two opposing players and neither one can free it.

4

Ready to Play

The first six players to start the game for each team comprise that team's *starting lineup*. Each player has a distinct position and a specific job to do. The six starting positions are: goalie, left defenseman, right defenseman, center, left wing, and right wing. The two defensemen make up the defensive line, and the center and the two wings make up the forward (offensive) line. In the NHL, a full team usually consists of two goalies and 18 other players. A team usually has four forward lines (12 players) and six defensemen. The other three or four players are spare forwards and/or defensemen.

If a player breaks the rules and commits a penalty, the team may have to play shorthanded, with only five (or even four) players instead of the full complement of six. The team that has the extra player is said to be on a *power play*, and the team that is shorthanded is said to be attempting to *kill the penalty*.

Positions on the Team

The Center

The center leads the team's attack when it is trying to score a goal. The center is also the player who takes part in most of the face-offs. The center starts the play on the forward line but can move anywhere on the ice in pursuit of the puck. A center must be able to control the puck well and pass it to the teammates who have the best goal-scoring opportunities. Good centers are usually able to score many goals and have a great number of assists.

Left and Right Wings

These members of the forward line skate on their respective sides of the rink, on either side of the center. They approach the goal from different sides of the ice, giving each a different angle from which to shoot at the goal. The wings pass the puck to each other and to the center to try to score goals. The wings are often the team's most prolific goal scorers. Depending on the coach's offensive strategy, the wings may crisscross the ice, irrespective of their starting positions.

Defensemen

The left and right defensemen are expected to defend their own goal, although not in the same way as the goalie. The left defenseman covers the left half of the rink, and the right defenseman plays to the right (but they too can crisscross the ice as necessary during play). The defensemen's job is to harass the attacking team's wings and centers, guard the area in front of the net, block shots and passes, and clear rebounds from in front of the goalie before the other team can score.

When their team is defending and their opponents have the puck, the defensemen will use checking and blocking techniques to try to steal the puck and make it impossible for the other team to continue its attack. Once the puck has crossed the blue line into the defensive zone, one defenseman will stand near the goal to cover the opposing team's forwards, while the other will go after the player controlling the puck.

When their team is on the attack, the defensemen will try to keep the puck in the other team's defensive zone by passing it to their teammates, or shooting on net. In this case, the defensemen are called "point men" or just "points," and they use a technique called *backchecking* to break up a sudden counterattack by the opposing team. They are positioned on the "points," on opposite sides of the ice near the opposing team's blue line.

The Goalie

Also called the goalkeeper, goaltender, or netminder, the goalie usually plays the entire game unless replaced for reasons of injury or ineptitude. The goalie has the only job that does not require skating all around the ice.

The goalie's responsibility is to stay near the team's goal and protect it. The goalie's area is the goal crease directly in front of the goal. The goalie usually stands in front of the goal with leg pads close together and knees bent, to allow rapid movement in either direction. The body is slightly bent forward at the waist. One hand holds the stick, keeping the blade flat on the ice in front of the goalie's skates; the other hand, wearing the catching glove, is ready to grab a flying puck.

The rules of hockey give the goalies distinct privileges. The goalie is the only player who can pick up or freeze the puck with the hands or body. Opposing players cannot make deliberate contact with the goalie either inside or outside the goal crease. The goalie tries in any way possible to stop the fast-moving puck, which may be traveling at 100 miles per hour or more. A goalie may stop a shot with the full body, by lying flat on the ice, or by using gloves, heavily padded arms, skates, or stick. The goalie may catch the puck and push it away, direct it toward a teammate, or hold onto it so the opposing team doesn't get another immediate chance to score.

Being a goalie is one of the hardest jobs in sports. The goalie must keep the other team from scoring until his or her teammates can regain the puck. Goalies must have very fast reflexes and must

Goalie standing guard

constantly be alert to what's going on during the game. The goalie must make sure he or she is watching the puck at all times, so the opponents don't get the opportunity to sneak in a goal.

Penalty Killers

Certain team members who are good at specific skills may be sent onto the ice as specialists. For example, the team may employ as a penalty killer a strong skating forward who is particularly good at defensive hockey, or at keeping and gaining control of a loose puck under difficult circumstances. Similarly, a defenseman with excellent checking and blocking skills may be used to kill penalties. The coach will turn to such players when the team is shorthanded, to defend against a power play.

Power Play Unit

Just as certain team members are used as penalty killers while killing a penalty, other team members are used as offensive specialists while on the power play. For example, teams will use players who excel at shooting and passing the puck. Some coaches will also use a high-scoring forward in a defensemen's position to help provide more offensive opportunities.

Team and Individual Scoring

A team wins a hockey game by scoring more goals than its opponents. A legal goal is scored when the puck is hit by the stick of an attacking player between the goal posts of the opponent's goal and crosses completely over the red goal line. In order for the goal to be legal, the puck must be hit while the stick is below shoulder level. A goal is not scored if the puck bounces off an official. The puck may not be kicked, batted by hand, or thrown into the net by an attacking player. The goal is legal, however, if a defender accidentally bumps the puck into the net, or if a shot by the attacking team goes into the net after being deflected by a defender.

A *hat trick* occurs when a player scores three or more goals in a single game. This is quite an accomplishment and usually results in fans throwing their hats onto the ice as a symbol of appreciation.

For the purpose of measuring individual performance, players are awarded points based on their total number of goals and assists. Both an assist and a goal are worth one point. When a player passes the puck to a teammate who scores, it is said that the passer has provided assistance, or an assist, to the goal scorer. On a play that involves more than one pass to set up a goal, two players may each be awarded an assist. Decisions as to who gets credit for goals and assists are made by the referee and official scorer.

After a goal is scored, the referee reports it to the official scorer. Then an announcement is usually made. For example, in the NHL you might hear: "Goal scored for the Colorado Avalanche by number 19, Joe Sakic, with assists from number 21, Peter Forsberg, and number 4, Rob Blake." A player can score a goal unassisted or with the help of one or two players.

A shot taken by an attacking player that would have been a goal if not saved by the goalie is called a *shot on goal* (SOG). A shot that hits the goalpost and bounces out is not officially a shot on goal. Goals scored also count as shots on goal.

Penalties

In hockey there are team penalties and individual penalties, which are called by the officials when a player or team breaks a rule. A team penalty often results in a face-off. There are six categories of individual penalties— minor, major, bench, match, misconduct, and penalty shot—each of which is treated differently. A player who commits a penalty must spend game time off the ice, except in the case of a penalty shot.

Unlike other sports in which any player may address an official, in ice hockey only the team captain, or alternate captains, may question or discuss with the officials anything relating to the rules or penalties. The captain's jersey will have a "C" sewn on, and the alternates will each have an "A." Any other player who discusses or protests a call with an official can be penalized for misconduct.

Sometimes penalties are given for actions that are meant to harm another player. Such aggression is dealt with severely and may result in a multiple-game suspension and, in the NHL, a severe fine.

Playing Rule Infractions

The following are common violations that result in a face-off but not in a power play for either team.

Offsides

Hockey rules require that attacking players must follow the puck into the attacking zone—the players are not allowed to get there first. The purpose of the offsides rule is to prevent an attacking player from standing in front of the opponent's goal and waiting for a long pass that would give the attacker an easy chance to score. An attacking player is considered offside if both skates go over the blue line into the attacking zone before the puck does. If only one skate is over the blue line, with the player straddling the line, the player is onside and there is no infraction. A face-off is held outside the attacking zone near the spot where the violation occurred.

A linesmen may signal a *delayed offsides* by raising an arm but not blowing the whistle and stopping the action until the outcome of the play is determined. For example, the linesmen may decide to wait to call the infraction because if the defense is able to get control of the puck, stopping the play would penalize the wrong team. If this happens, the offsides is waved off or canceled by the linesmen, and play continues uninterrupted.

Center Line Offsides Pass

The center line offsides pass is another type of offsides violation, but used only in the NHL. It occurs when a player, who has preceded the puck over the center red line, receives a pass from a teammate that originated in his defending zone. A face-off is held at the spot where the pass initiating the violation occurred.

Icing

An icing violation occurs when the team that has the puck shoots toward the opponent's goal from behind the red center line and the puck goes into the end of the rink across the red goal line, but not into the goal. In international and Olympic games, icing is called immediately when the puck crosses the goal line; in the NHL, icing is called when a member of the opposing team touches the puck first. A face-off is then held in the penalized team's defensive zone. It is not icing if the puck goes into the goal.

In all of ice hockey, icing is *never* called against a shorthanded team. Nor is icing called if the puck is touched by the goalie, or if a member of the attacking team touches it first.

Individual Penalties and Shorthanded Play

When a player violates certain rules, that player is punished by removal from play. The player is then forced to sit on the penalty bench in the penalty box and miss actual playing time. This leaves the penalized players' team with one less player on the ice. The penalized team must play shorthanded unless the other team has a player in the penalty box as well.

Most individual penalties are called when a player interferes with an opponent, deliberately tries to harm another player, or plays in a dangerous manner. When a penalty is called, play stops and the penalized player leaves the ice. Play restarts with a face-off, which is usually held near where the action was stopped.

A team may have to play two players down if two penalties are called on players of the same team, or if one player is already in the penalty box from a prior penalty when a second team member in penalized. There is no practical limit on the number of penalties or the amount of penalty time that can be called against a team. However, regardless of how many penalties are called, a team may not have fewer than four players on the ice (including the goalie).

Delayed Penalties

Penalties that would cause a team to play with fewer than four players become *delayed penalties* and are served when the other penalties expire. Delayed penalties are served in the order they were assessed. When a team is penalized for a third time, and two teammates are already in the penalty box, the third penalized player joins his two teammates in the penalty box, and a substitute player goes out onto the ice. This hurts the team in many ways. Even though the team has the same number of players on the ice, when the penalties are finished, instead of rejoining the game immediately, the penalized players must remain in the penalty box until the first stoppage of play or until the next penalty expires, whichever comes first. Only then can they go back to the team bench, after which they may reenter the game as substitutes during a line change or for the next face-off. Any time remaining on a penalty when the period ends is carried over into the next period.

A second type of delayed penalty arises when a penalty is called against a player on the team that is not in possession of the puck. When a penalty is called on a player on the team that has possession of the puck, the whistle is blown and the play stops immediately. When a player not on a team in possession of the puck causes a penalty, however, the referee will point to the offending player and will wait for the team with possession of the puck to complete its play either with a goal or loss of possession. The purpose of the delay is to allow the non-offending team in possession of the puck to score a goal. If the penalty is minor and the non-offending team scores a goal, often the penalty will not be imposed on the offending team. Major penalties are always imposed—even if a goal is scored.

Minor Penalties

A player who commits a minor penalty sits in the penalty box for two minutes. However, if the attacking team scores on a power play when a player is in the penalty box and the defending team is shorthanded, the player can return to the ice after the goal is scored even if the full penalty time has not been served.

The most common minor penalties endanger an opponent or improperly impede that player's progress. The minor offenses include interference, tripping, boarding, cross-checking, slashing, charging, elbowing, holding, high-sticking, hooking, closing the hand on the puck, playing with a broken stick, deliberately falling on the puck, holding the puck against the boards when not being checked, leaving the bench illegally, and roughing. A player may also be penalized for faking an action or "taking a dive" in order to draw an unwarranted penalty call on the other team.

Double minors, which total four minutes in the penalty box, are assessed either for an accidental infraction that results in an injury or for an apparent attempt to injure a player that does not result in an injury. These infractions are more serious than a minor penalty but less serious than a major penalty. If the opposing team scores during a double minor, only one of the minor penalties is deducted from the player's time in the penalty box.

Major Penalties

Major penalties are often assessed for the same infractions as minor penalties, except that in the case of a major penalty the official believes the penalized player acted either with a greater degree of violence or with deliberate violence against the opponent. When what would ordinarily be a minor penalty is committed but blood is drawn, a major penalty may be assessed.

In a major penalty, the penalized player spends five minutes in the penalty box, and there is no premature return to the ice even if a goal is scored. Fighting and spearing are two infractions that always result in major penalties. Other infractions such as boarding or hitting from behind very often result in major penalties because of the likelihood of injury.

Common Individual Penalties

Listed below are some common penalties and how they are committed.

- **Boarding**—When a player violently pushes an opponent into the boards by body checking, elbowing, or tripping.

- **Charging**—When a player deliberately moves by more than two steps to run into an opponent. Charging is also called when a player leaves his or her feet and jumps into an opponent to check that player.

- **Cross-checking**—When a player with both hands on the stick and no part of the stick on the ice uses the stick to check an opponent.

- **Delay of game**—When a player purposely delays the game in any way (for example, by shooting or batting the puck outside the playing area, or deliberately displacing the goal post from its normal position) in order to get the referee to stop play.

- **Elbowing**—When a player strikes an opponent with an elbow.

- **Falling on the puck**—When a player falls on the puck and gathers it close to the body or puts his or her hands around it.

- **Fighting**—When opposing players engage in an altercation. If a referee decides that one player instigated the fight, that player can receive extra penalties, or even a game misconduct.

- **High-sticking**—When a player checks an opponent while holding the stick above the level of the opponent's waist.

- **Holding**—When one player holds onto or wraps his or her arms around an opponent or the opponent's stick to block the opponent's progress.

- **Hooking**—When a player tries to impede the progress of the opponent by hooking the opponent with the blade of the stick.

- **Interference**—When a player tries to stop or impede the motion of another player who is not in possession of the puck.

- **Kneeing**—When a player hits an opponent with the knee.

- **Roughing**—When a player is involved in a minor altercation, usually consisting of shoving and pushing.

- **Slashing**—When a player swings his or her stick in a slashing motion at the opponent.

- **Spearing**—When a player uses the stick like a spear or bayonet against an opponent.

- **Too many men on the ice**—When a substitute leaves the bench while play continues, and comes onto the ice prematurely. In the NHL, players may be changed at any time from the players' bench, provided that the player or players leaving the ice are within five feet of the bench and out of the play before the change is made.

- **Tripping**—When a player trips an opponent with his or her stick or body.

- **Unsportsmanlike conduct**—When a player argues with a referee, or acts in an unprofessional manner.

Bench Penalties

Bench penalties occur when anyone on the bench commits an infraction. Such infractions can include using improper language with an official, throwing something onto the ice, improperly leaving the bench, or doing anything to interfere with the game or one of the officials. A bench penalty can also be assessed for making an improper change to the starting lineup or for an illegal substitution (such as having too many players on the ice at one time during play). If that happens, one of the players on the ice must spend two minutes in the penalty box.

Game Misconduct or Match Penalties

Game misconduct or match penalties are rare, and are the most severe penalties that can be called by an official. They call for banishment of a player from the game and possibly a suspension or a fine.

A game misconduct penalty is imposed when one player deliberately injures another. The offending player must leave the game, and a substitute must sit in the penalty box for however many penalty minutes were assessed, leaving the team shorthanded.

Misconduct Penalties

Misconduct penalties differ from other penalties in that they allow immediate substitution, and the team does not have to play shorthanded. However, the penalized player may not return to the ice for at least ten minutes. A misconduct penalty is often given for abusive language or gestures, failure to follow an official's orders, showing disrespect for a ruling, knocking or shooting the puck out of the reach of an official who is trying to retrieve it, throwing equipment onto the ice, banging the boards with the stick, not proceeding to the penalty box when instructed to do so, ignoring a warning to stop trying to incite another player into a penalty, or other unsportsmanlike conduct.

Penalty Shot

A penalty shot is one of the rarest and most exciting plays in hockey. In a penalty shot, an attacking player is allowed to move the puck from center ice into the attacking zone and go one-on-one against the goalie in an attempt to score, while the other players stand behind the red center line. The puck is placed on the center face-off spot, and the player can stickhandle it anywhere, as long as continuing toward the goal, to set up the shot. Only one shot is allowed, and a rebound shot does not count.

The referee awards a penalty shot to a player who has been illegally prevented from capitalizing on a scoring opportunity. This can occur when a player is interfered with from behind while on a breakaway, when a defensemen deliberately falls on the puck in the goal crease, or when a player deliberately throws a stick to interfere with play. Generally, the fouled player gets to take the penalty shot.

Goalie Penalties

When a goalie commits a penalty, the netminder is usually allowed to remain in the game; a teammate on the ice will head for the penalty box to serve the goalie's time. But if the goalie commits three major penalties, the netminder will get a game misconduct penalty and will be forced to leave the game, just like any other player. Similarly, a goalie who gets a match penalty must also leave the game. In such cases, a substitute goalie comes in.

If the goalie holds onto the puck when there are no opposing players around to check him, or if the goalie deliberately uses his stick to shoot the puck out of the rink, the goalie will be called for a delay of game penalty.

Coincidental Penalties

Coincidental penalties occur when an equal number of players on both teams must serve the same number of major or minor penalties of equal length at the same time. When each team is hit with a minor penalty, the two players serve their time, without substitution, as in a normal penalty situation. But when coincidental penalties are called on more than one player on each team, they cancel each other out. Although the penalized players must go into the penalty box, substitute players immediately come onto the ice. This is to keep teams from having fewer than five players on the ice. Once the penalty time has expired, the players can return to the ice only after play has stopped.

Boarding

Body Checking

Butt-Ending

Charging

Checking from
Behind

Cross Checking

Delayed (Slow)
Whistle

Delayed Calling
of Penalty

Delay of Game A

Delay of Game B

Elbowing

Fighting/
Roughing

Goal Scored

Hand Pass

High Sticking

Holding the
Face Mask

Holding

Hooking

Icing

Interference

Kneeing

Match Penalty

Misconduct

Penalty Shot

Slashing

Spearing

Time Out

Tripping

Washout

The Power Play

When one team is playing shorthanded, the other team gets a chance to employ what is called a *power play*. In a power play, the team with more players on the ice tries to move all of its players, except the goalie, to the opposing team's defensive zone. From this location, they will take shot after shot at the goal, trying to overwhelm the opposing goalie.

Members of the shorthanded team, meanwhile, try to kill the penalty—that is, they try to keep from being scored on until they are back at full strength. To do this, the shorthanded team sends in penalty killers, experts who are adept at taking the puck away from the opponents and whose excellent defensive and stickhandling abilities can help the goalie protect the goal.

5

Hockey Strategies

Playing hockey is lots of fun, but it can sometimes be difficult to follow because of its very fast action. Here are some strategies to employ and tips to keep in mind as you play or watch the action.

- *Watch the puck.* In hockey, the puck often ricochets off the boards after hard shots or passes. You always need to anticipate how the puck will carom, or rebound. Many hockey players use the boards like the bumpers on a pool table. You need to figure out where the puck will land after it hits the boards, and get there first.

- *Pay attention to the matchups.* A matchup is a pairing of players from opposing teams who cover each other throughout the game. Covering a player means making sure that player doesn't successfully receive the puck and make a play on offense. In the NHL, matchups are extremely important, and the home team always has the edge: the visiting team must name its starting line first, so the home team gets to match up the players to its advantage.

- *Watch for the attack patterns.* Players can quickly skate from one end of the rink to the other; when the attackers skate together toward the opponent's goal, this is called a break or a rush. A break is designed to catch the other team's defense off guard, and it gives the rushing team a better chance to score. Situations often develop in which the attackers rushing up ice outnumber the defenders in the attacking zone. If two attackers are guarded by only one defenseman, this is called a two-on-one break. The more outnumbered the defensemen, the better the chance the attackers will have a player open for a shot on goal. The best example of a break is the *breakaway*, in which an attacker with the puck skates undefended toward the goal. This is similar to a penalty shot, in which a lone attacker goes against the goalie in a one-to-one showdown.

Attack Strategies
Dumping the Puck into the Zone
Because of the offsides rules, attackers must be careful not to go into the attacking zone until the puck has crossed the blue line.

Clive Brunskill/ALLSPORT

A Finnish player crashes into the boards as Darby Hendrickson of Team USA attacks during the 1994 Winter Olympics in Lillehammer.

Brian Bahr/ALLSPORT

Chris Drury of the Colorado Avalanche dekes and slides the puck
past goalie Martin Brodeur of the New Jersey Devils
during the Stanley Cup finals.

When one or more attacking players are about to commit an
offsides violation, often one player will dump or shoot the puck
into the attacking zone, where a teammate will chase after the
puck and try to regain control of it before the opposing goalie
or defensemen can take possession.

Deking

A deke (short for "decoy") is a move made by the puck carrier
to fool the defender into thinking the opponent is going to
pass or move in one particular direction rather than another.
Body control and stickhandling are key to successful deking. A
defender should always watch the opponent's chest, because it
usually gives away the player's true intentions.

There are three main types of dekes:

- **Shoulder deke**—The shoulder moves in one direction but
  the player in another.

- **Head deke**—A player drops the head as if moving one way but actually moves in the opposite direction.

- **Stick deke**—The stick is moved as if for a shot, but instead the player moves the puck past the defenseman.

Where to Shoot the Puck in the Net

Players usually try to shoot the puck at areas of the net that are the most difficult for the goalie to defend. The most popular areas that players aim for are the upper and lower left and right corners and between the goalie's legs, called the "five-hole." Since most goalies are usually slower with their feet than with their hands, it is better to shoot for the lower corners, since the goalie has to use the feet or stick to defend those areas. Higher shots, which are a little easier for the goalie to defend, should be taken when the goalie is kneeling or lying on the ice.

Screening the Goalie

Goalies usually have quick reflexes and good eyesight and can see shots easily from close range. Often players on an attacking team try to stand in front of the goalie to block or screen the goalie's line of vision. This tactic works because when a goalie cannot see the puck coming until the very last instant, he or she has less time to react and make a save. Remember, though, that players on the attacking team are not allowed to stand in the goal crease.

Deflections

The same players who effectively screen the goalie are also in a good position to use their sticks to deflect a shot or a pass into the net. When the goalie anticipates the direction of the puck from the shooter's stick, the goalie cannot react in time to stop a deflection that changes the puck's direction.

Jamie Squire/ALLSPORT

Forward Geoff Courtnall of the St. Louis Blues attempts to
screen goalkeeper Nikolai Khabibulin of the Phoenix Coyotes
as they scramble for the loose puck while defenseman
Oleg Tverdovsky prepares to clear the zone.

Defense Strategies

Defense players try to stop the attacking players and knock the
puck away any way they can. The best defenders do this with
their skating skill, stickhandling ability, and hard legal checking.

Rather than concentrating on knocking the puck away with
the stick, a good defenseman, covering a player, often checks
the opponent repeatedly, to make sure the attacker cannot get
off a good pass or shot. A defenseman who only goes after the
puck is taking a risk, because if the puck is missed, the attacking
player may get around the defender and have an open lane for
a pass or a goal.

Goalie Strategies

Cutting Down the Angle

When an attacker is skating with the puck toward the goal, the goalie will often skate several feet out in front of the net. This cuts down the angle of the attacker's shot, leaving the attacker with less net area to hit. From the goalie's viewpoint, this aggressive strategy can be very effective. The risk is that if the attacker gets past the goalie, the attacker will have an easy shot at the empty net.

Pulling the Goalie

When a team is losing by a few goals near the end of the game and desperately needs to score, the coach will often "pull" the goalie. The idea is that by removing the goalie, the team can get another potential goal scorer out on the ice.

This replacement player has none of the duties of a goalie and none of the privileges. The player cannot handle the puck like the goalie, nor is he protected from contact. This desperation tactic is used to get more scoring power on the ice in the final minutes of the game, so the team can catch up or win. It leaves the team's goal unguarded, and that open net gives the other team an opportunity to score easily if it gains possession of the puck. This type of goal is called an *empty-net goal.*

Power Plays

A power play, in which one team has more players on the ice than the other, is an excellent scoring opportunity. The strategies for a power play are a little different than those for when the teams are at equal strength.

Power Play Setup

The team with the extra player tries to get set up in the attacking zone. Here it will always have one more player who is open and not being defended. The only way the team on the power play can take advantage of this opportunity is by moving the puck around the attacking zone and working to get clear shots on goal.

After setting up in the attacking zone, the players pass the puck quickly, trying to find the attacker with the best open shot. The defensemen on the power play team set up at the points, just inside the blue line, from which they can shoot at the net or pass to their teammates. The players at the points also work to keep the puck inside the zone. If the puck does leave the zone, all the attacking players must clear the attacking zone, in order to prevent an offsides call, before the puck can be brought back in.

Shorthanded Strategy

The team with fewer players (the shorthanded team) attempts to hold off the attack by trying to regain the puck and keep it away from the power play team as long as possible. The shorthanded team tries to kill the penalty by holding the puck until the penalty time winds down or expires. When the attacking team is set up in the attacking zone, the defending team always tries to clear the puck or shoot it out of its defending zone. This forces the attacking team to set up its power play all over again. A shorthanded team cannot be called for icing, so players in this situation will often slap the puck out of their own defending zone as hard as they can in order to kill time on the penalty.

6

Nutrition and Health

Good health is important for anyone who competes in any sport, but it is particularly important to be in good shape to play the fast-paced game of ice hockey. A major fringe benefit of hockey is that the good health and fitness habits you develop while learning and training for ice hockey will carry over to any other sport or recreational activity you enjoy.

Good Eating Habits

Good eating habits go hand-in-hand with fitness training. You can be in good health without being physically fit, but you can't become physically fit without eating a well-balanced diet that contains protein, fats, and carbohydrates in the proper amounts. A healthy nutritional program for Americans was proposed years ago when the U.S. Department of Agriculture (USDA) and the Department of Health and Human Services (DHHS) published detailed guidelines for a good diet. The guidelines were issued in revised form in May 2000. These guidelines emphasize the importance of carbohydrates and the less important role of protein and fats in a healthful nutrition program.

Carbohydrates are sugars and starches that appear in two forms—either simple or complex. The simple form, found in processed foods such as candy, soft drinks, or sweet desserts, should be avoided. These provide only "empty" calories, low-quality nutrients that may taste good momentarily but do nothing for overall health. It's not necessary to eliminate them entirely from your diet, but be selective. (Your dentist will be happy, too.) Sugar, in its natural form, is abundant in fresh fruit, and a good way to satisfy a sweet tooth is by eating a piece of fruit instead of a candy bar.

Snacking in front of the television set seems to be a common American dietary habit. For the athlete who is serious about ice hockey and getting fit, however, there is no place for high-fat, high-salt, high-calorie "junk food" in the diet. Try munching on an apple, a tangerine, or carrot and celery sticks when you watch your favorite show or when you need a snack during the day.

Complex carbohydrates are an athlete's best nutritional friends because they are a primary source of fuel. You'll find them in bread, vegetables of all colors (especially peas and beans), fruit, nuts, pasta, and whole grains (wheat, rice, corn, and oats). They should make up about 60 percent of your daily food intake.

Protein is found in several foods—nuts, dairy products, and lean meats, poultry, and low-fat fish. A 16-ounce T-bone steak every day isn't needed to "build muscle." In fact, that's probably too much protein for your body to absorb efficiently; the rest just goes to waste. Try to keep your protein consumption to about 20 percent of what you eat each day, and you'll consume enough to build muscle, maintain it, and repair it when necessary.

Your body does need some fat, but not nearly as much as most Americans consume every day from a diet that is often overloaded with fat and salt. The fat you eat should come from margarine, vegetable oil, or nuts and should be no more than 20 percent of your daily intake of food. Fat has some benefits—it is an insulator in cold weather and an energy source—but a little goes a long way in keeping an athlete healthy and fit.

A Guide to Daily Food Choices

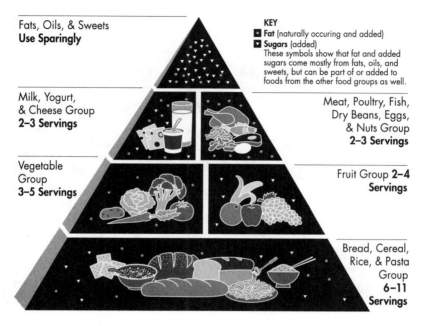

Fats, Oils, & Sweets
Use Sparingly

KEY
■ **Fat** (naturally occuring and added)
▼ **Sugars** (added)
These symbols show that fat and added sugars come mostly from fats, oils, and sweets, but can be part of or added to foods from the other food groups as well.

Milk, Yogurt,
& Cheese Group
2–3 Servings

Meat, Poultry, Fish,
Dry Beans, Eggs,
& Nuts Group
2–3 Servings

Vegetable
Group
3–5 Servings

Fruit Group **2–4
Servings**

Bread, Cereal,
Rice, & Pasta
Group
**6–11
Servings**

Source: U.S. Department of Agriculture and the
U.S. Department of Health and Human Services

Don't skip meals—especially breakfast. Breakfast is like putting gas in your car—you need it to get started—and that meal should be a good, solid one-third of your daily calorie intake. Not hungry for breakfast in the morning? Try this once: eat a light dinner the night before. You'll have an appetite in the morning that will help you get on a regular meal schedule. Eating breakfast will make you feel better all day.

There is no nutritional law that requires a "traditional" breakfast. There is nothing wrong with eating a baked potato, having a healthy soup, or eating lean meat, fish, or poultry at your first meal of the day. The important point is to learn to eat well-balanced, nutritious meals throughout the day, starting with the first one.

Elsa Hasch /ALLSPORT

Drinking plenty of water is the key to staying hydrated.

A word on liquids: Avoid cola drinks, coffee, and tea. They are high in caffeine, which acts as a diuretic to take water from your body. The one liquid you should not avoid is water, which is 60 percent of your body's weight and is needed to lubricate your joints and maintain your body's temperature. Water is also the transportation system for the nutrients you need to stay healthy, so don't neglect this crucial liquid. One or two quarts per day will keep your body well lubricated and prevent dehydration.

The new dietary guidelines from the USDA and the DHHS suggest that Americans "… limit the intake of beverages and foods that are high in added sugars." For example, a Food and Drug Administration (FDA) study published in early 2000 reported that soda consumption per person in the United States had reached 41 gallons in 1997. This is nearly double the 1970 rate of consumption of 22 gallons. A 12-ounce can of soda contains nine teaspoons of sugar, an amount that you could visualize by measuring the amount into a cup or glass.

The sizes of soda containers have kept pace with consumption, from the standard 6.5-ounce bottle of the 1950s to today's 12-, 20-, and 64-ounce containers. As soda consumption has gone up, milk, juice, and water consumption has gone down. Sodas are high-calorie drinks that don't contain the vitamins and minerals needed for good health, so limiting your consumption is probably a good idea.

A recent study at Harvard University of adolescent girls (whose bones are maturing) indicates that many are drinking more sodas, not eating calcium-rich foods, and not getting enough weight-bearing exercise, such as running or tennis. Over time, these dietary and exercise deficits can lead to thin, brittle bones that fracture easily.

The problem is of such concern that the DHHS, the Centers for Disease Control (CDC), and the National Osteoporosis Foundation are cooperating on an information campaign aimed at girls between the ages of 9 and 12. The campaign will stress the importance of calcium in the diet, which foods are good sources of calcium, and the importance of combining weight-bearing exercise with calcium intake.

The dietary guidelines also make statements about exercise and sodium (salt) in the diet. For the first time, Americans are urged to include "moderate daily exercise" of at least 30 minutes per day in their lifestyles and to "…choose and prepare foods with less salt." This means avoiding soy sauce, ketchup, mustard, pickles, and olives.

Finally, there are no "miracle foods" or "miracle diets" or "miracle pills" that will keep you in perfect health and physically fit. A well-balanced diet, paired with regular exercise, will help you stay in shape for life.

Precautions

Tobacco

Approximately 40–50 million Americans smoke, and studies have shown that most of them began in their early teens. The number of cigarettes smoked and the percentage of smokers have declined steadily over the last 15 years, but occasional "social" smoking is up. "Social" smokers have a sense that smoking is not harmful to their health and that they are not likely to become addicted, even though the contrary is true.

It is estimated that 4.5 million adolescents (aged 11–17) are cigarette smokers. Each day, more than 6,000 people under 18 years old try a cigarette for the first time; each day, smoking becomes a daily habit for more than 3,000 people under 18 years of age. It cannot be said too often: the use of tobacco is addictive.

Cigarette smoking during adolescence leads to significant health problems, including respiratory illnesses, decreased physical fitness, and retardation in lung growth and function.

Based on recent statistical evidence from the Tobacco Intervention Network, large numbers of young males are becoming addicted to smokeless tobacco, apparently in an effort to imitate professional athletes or to conform to peer pressure. Smokeless tobacco causes dental cavities—it is one-third sugar—and the irritation caused by holding a wad of tobacco in the mouth causes receding gums, gum disease, bone loss, and the inevitable tooth loss.

All drugs have side effects, and smokeless tobacco is no exception. It increases blood pressure and heart rate, and seems to increase the likelihood of kidney disease. Smokeless tobacco does not improve an athlete's reaction time. Both the National Institute of Drug Abuse and the American Psychological Association agree that smokeless tobacco can produce dependency and result in addiction.

The use of any tobacco product by hockey officials is not strictly prohibited, but it is certainly not recommended. Coaches, players, and team personnel at the high school level can be found guilty of unsportsmanlike conduct if they use tobacco products.

Marijuana

The Partnership for a Drug-Free America believes that marijuana smoking among teens has reached epidemic proportions Many youngsters think smoking marijuana is not dangerous, and that it is a "safe" alternative to alcohol or tobacco. One reason for this misconception is that because there was less marijuana smoking in the 1980s, many young people have not seen "pothead burnout" among adults or their peers and are ignorant of the consequences.

The ramifications of smoking marijuana have not been publicized, but 30 years of research have pinpointed the effects. According to Monika Guttman, who writes extensively about drug use, "marijuana reduces coordination; slows reflexes; interferes with the ability to measure distance, speed and time; and disrupts concentration and short-term memory." (Everything listed would be detrimental to any athlete, especially an ice hockey player.)

Marijuana has six times as many carcinogens (cancer-causing agents) as tobacco. Today's marijuana is much more potent, creates dependency faster, and often becomes an "entrance" drug—one that can lead to dependence on "hard" drugs such as cocaine.

Currently, nearly 12.5 million Americans use illegal drugs, and teenagers are the fastest-growing segment of first-time illegal drug users. Teens, especially, know that drugs are the most important problem they face—ahead of violence, sex issues, and getting into college. They need a clear message about dangerous, illegal, and unhealthy drugs.

Drug-prevention materials for young people and adults are available by contacting the U.S. Anti-Doping Agency at 1-800-233-0393 or via the Internet at http://www.usantidoping.org.

Steroids

Some types of drugs have been used by athletes for many years. Athletes —even Olympic athletes—sometimes say they take drugs to win medals. Perhaps that is why these drugs have been misnamed "performance enhancing," when in reality they are not. Steroids, amphetamines, hormones, human growth hormone (hGH), and erythropoietin (EPO) are a few drugs specifically banned by the International Olympic Committee (IOC).

The American Medical Association (AMA), U.S. Anti-Doping Agency (USADA), World Anti-Doping Agency (WADA), and National Collegiate Athletic Association (NCAA) have deplored the use of steroids for muscle building or improved athletic performance. Steroids (anabolic-androgenic steroids, or AAS) are a drug danger, with terrible consequences for the user.

The food additive androstenedione, or "andro," has been identified as a steroid. The USADA, WADA, and NCAA, along with other sports organizations, have banned its use by athletes.

Steroid abuse is an increasing problem in teenagers. Steroid use by males can result in breast development, hair loss, and acne, plus yellow skin and eyes. For females, breasts shrink, hair grows on the face and body, and menstrual cycles can become irregular. For both, the result of steroid use can be a permanent stunting of bone growth and can cause permanent damage to the heart, liver, and kidneys. Steroid abuse raises the risk of strokes and blood clots.

The psychological effects of steroid use are just as devastating, according to the American Sports Education Institute, which has noted the following: "Wide mood swings ranging from periods of violent, even homicidal, episodes known as 'roid rages' to depression, paranoid jealousy, extreme irritability, delusions, and impaired judgment."

Effects of using EPO can range from sterility to the risk of heart attack, liver and kidney disease, and some cancers. EPO and amphetamines have caused deaths in athletes, and the long-term affects on a normal-sized person of using human growth hormones are still unknown.

A partial list of the consequences of taking any of these drugs is as follows:

- Creatine: Side effects are dizziness, diarrhea, and cramps.

- EPO: Forces the heart to work harder; can cause heart attacks, strokes, and sudden death.

- Anabolic steroids: Higher cholesterol, "roid rages," perhaps liver disease and cancer, heart disease, brain tumors. Among women, hair on the face, lost hair from the head, acne, breast shrinkage, and cessation of menstrual periods.

- Cyproterone acetate: Stops sexual development in women.

- Human growth hormone (hGH): Side effects are unusual bone growth (acromegaly); forehead, cheeks, jaw, hands, and feet grow grotesquely.

- Amphetamines: Temporary boosters that increase heart rate, blood pressure, and respiration. They do not boost performance levels; in fact, they actually decrease them.

In addition to steroids, the World Anti-Doping Agency prohibits hundreds of substances that can enhance athletic performance. For more information on banned substances, contact:

The World Anti-Doping Agency (WADA)
http://www.wada-ama.org

Vision Care

If you wear corrective lenses and want to play ice hockey, talk to your eye doctor and ask the specialist if contact lenses would be suitable for you. Today's contacts come in hard and soft materials and are lightweight, and some can be worn for hours at a time. In fact, there are disposable contact lenses that can be worn 24 hours a day, don't require special cleaning, and can be disposed of after seven days. The latter are fairly expensive, however, and may not be suitable for the young, growing athlete. Always check with your eye doctor and follow the doctor's recommendations for your needs. If you wear traditional contacts, be sure to have your cleaning and wetting solutions with you at practices and games, and to let your coach know you wear contacts.

7

Physical Fitness

It's never too soon, or too late, to begin exercising and getting your body into good working order. If you are overweight, get winded easily, or are otherwise out of shape, you may have difficulty participating in ice hockey games. Consult your physician, however, before beginning any fitness program, and work only under the supervision of a qualified, knowledgeable trainer or coach.

Coaches can test the fitness of their players—either rookies or veterans—with a few simple exercises done in preseason. This allows time to work on improving fitness.

- *Strength and balance*: The player stands on one side of a bench and grasps the top with both hands. Then, while holding the top with both hands and keeping the feet together, the player jumps over the bench.

- *Hand speed*: Mark three spots on a smooth surface, e.g., a tabletop. Have the player keep one hand on the middle spot and use the other hand to tap spots on either side. Alternate the hand on the center spot.

- *Strength*: Have the player do sit-ups from a bent-knee position.

- *Balance*: Have the player stand on one leg and raise the free leg so that it is straight and parallel to the floor.

- *Coordination and agility*: With the feet together, have the player jump over a line from side-to-side.

- *Flexibility*: Have the player sit on the floor with legs outstretched. Then, have the player reach forward to touch the shins, ankles, toes, or soles of the feet.

The Four Parts of Fitness

Physical fitness has four parts: *muscle strength, muscle endurance, cardiovascular endurance* (heart, lungs, and blood vessels), and *flexibility.* Each part depends on the others to maintain physical fitness. Push-ups, for example, build strong muscles through repetition. Muscle endurance exercises aim to work muscles over a period of time without tiring them. Muscles need oxygen to function at peak levels, and this is why the heart, lungs, and blood vessels are so important to physical fitness. They sustain working muscles over long periods of time during practices and competitions.

Muscle Strength

Muscle strength can prevent aches and pains, keep the body aligned properly, and prevent injuries. Building this muscle strength requires fast and long exercise. The muscle gets "tired," but this is what builds strength. Muscles should feel a little uncomfortable, but not painful. The goal is overall muscle strength, since too much strength in one group of muscles could lead to an injury in another group. Strong muscles with low flexibility can lead to muscle pulls, while flexibility with low muscle strength can lead to dislocations.

Whether you use handheld dumbbells or sophisticated exercise machines, strength training techniques work the same way— they pit your muscles against resistance. Regular muscle strength training builds strength and endurance, helps with flexibility, and can help control weight. It can also increase your muscle mass and make you look good, but only if you work hard and are patient. Strength training takes time and effort.

A strength training session includes exercises for all the major muscle groups. Regular muscle training means working out at least twice a week, working between six and eight major muscle groups, and doing from one to three sets of 8–12 repetitions each.

Below are some basic strength training tips.

- **Warm up and cool down.** Make sure to get into the proper mental and physical state. Most workout injuries can be avoided with a 15-minute warmup. If you work out cold, you risk injury, but if you warm up and work out, you can stretch and grow.

- **Get off to a good start.** Make sure to start at your correct level. You risk injury if you set your sights too high on the first few days. A rule of thumb for weights is: if you can't lift the starting weight at least 15 to 18 times without loss of correct form, then you need to reduce the weight. The last two or three repetitions should be difficult, but not impossible.

- **Use proper technique.** If you want to maximize the benefits of training and minimize the risk of injury, make sure to use proper technique. You should work your muscles through the full range of motion. Without locking your joints, lift at a speed that permits you to control the weight and maintain good posture. Make sure you lift with a buddy spotting you.

- **Exercise large muscles first.** Your large muscles will be the first to fatigue, so work them first. Work the shoulders, legs, and chest before you go to the biceps, triceps, and lesser muscle groups.

- **Progress gradually.** Increase the number of repetitions before increasing weight or resistance. Reduce the rest interval between sets to increase the workload.

- **Breathe right.** Unless you are specifically told so elsewhere, exhale at the moment of highest exertion. Never hold your breath.

- **Challenge your muscles.** Start slow and work up with sets and reps for lasting benefits. Gradually increase weights until goals are reached. Modify the workout after you hit your plateau or meet your goals.

- **Take a break.** Rest and relax—rest is as important as the workout!

Muscle Endurance

Muscle endurance exercises build stamina and help the body perform at its best during a fast-paced, very physical hockey game. This type of training repeats the same exercise many times, using a relatively light weight. Aerobic exercises such as jogging, bicycling, and swimming are excellent for achieving muscle endurance. They also increase heart and lung efficiency and improve an athlete's personal appearance. Muscle endurance training should be done only three times a week because muscle fibers tear slightly during exercise and need time to rebuild themselves.

Cardiovascular Endurance

Cardiovascular endurance is achieved through exercises performed for at least 20 minutes. Walking, running, jogging, bicycling, swimming, dancing, and skipping rope are activities that raise the heart rate, take oxygen into the body, and move it to the muscles, which then provide the energy for the exercise being done.

Stationary bicycles are widely available and can be ridden to fit any personal schedule. Other indoor endurance exercises include jogging in place and doing jumping jacks or side hops. When exercising on a rug, wear gym socks; on a hard floor, shoes that cushion the feet are best.

Flexibility

There are numerous flexibility exercises—bends, stretches, swings, twists, lifts, raisers—that stretch out muscles that have "tightened" from vigorous exercise, such as a hockey game. Muscle-pull injuries are common when flexibility is poor.

Stretching and Warming Up

Regardless of your age, it is important that your body be flexible and relaxed. Loose muscles are not as susceptible to harm as tight muscles are. Maintaining flexibility is crucial to hockey success. One of the best ways to maintain flexibility and relax muscles is to stretch every day, even on the days without practice or a game. Skaters who fail to stretch regularly will most often suffer leg or shoulder injuries.

The point of stretching is to get the blood flowing and to loosen the muscles and tendons. Proper stretching should routinely include the neck, shoulders, back, and legs, including the upper

Robert Laberge/ALLSPORT

Jamie Storr of the Los Angeles Kings stretches his legs on the ice before a game.

and lower groin area. Stretching exercises should start at the neck and work down to the legs. Hold stretches for about six to ten seconds each. Release for a count of six, then repeat five times, at least twice a day. Remember to drink plenty of fluids when you stretch, especially in warm weather. The body's lymph nodes need fluid to carry away impurities, and without sufficient fluids the circulatory system cannot function effectively.

Neck

It is important to stretch the neck as much as possible and to loosen your neck muscles without rotation. The first neck stretch involves grabbing the back of your head with your right hand and pulling your head forward to the right. Repeat the process with your left hand. In the next stretch, raise your arms head-high, with elbows pointing out and away. Next, join your hands together behind your head and interlock your fingers. With your hands still behind your head, pull your head forward and down toward your chest.

Back

Lie on your back and press your knees into your chest, holding your shinbones with your hands. Release and repeat. Next, lie on your back with your arms stretched out perpendicular to your body. While turning your head to the right to look at your right hand, pull your right knee close to your chest and try to touch it to the ground on the left side of your body. Repeat the process on the left side.

Shoulders

Raise both your shoulders toward your ears while keeping your arms at your sides. Once shrugged, move your shoulders backward in slow, deliberate circles. Repeat the process in a forward motion.

Calf and Achilles Tendon

Stand about a foot from the wall, then extend one leg behind you, keeping both feet flat on the floor, toes pointed straight ahead, and your rear knee straight. Move your hips forward, keeping your lower back flat. Lean into the wall until you feel tension in the calf muscle of the extended leg. Hold for ten seconds, then stretch the other leg. Repeat the process a few times.

Hamstring

Stand and cross your right foot in front of your left. Lace your fingers behind your back. Slowly lower your forehead to your right knee, raising arms as you go. Repeat with your other leg. Alternatively, standing about a foot from the wall, place your hands on the wall at shoulder height, about shoulder width apart. Take a step back while pushing into the wall. Keep your back straight and press your back heel into the floor.

Quadriceps

Stand on your left leg. Reach back and hold your right foot behind you with your right hand. Balance against a wall with your left (free) hand as you pull gently upward on your right foot. If you do this correctly, you should feel a stretch in your right thigh, not in the knee. Switch legs and repeat.

Elsa Hasch/ALLSPORT

**Goalie Joe Blackburn of Team USA warms up before the
World Junior Hockey Championships.**

Motor Fitness

Motor fitness includes coordination, speed, balance, and agility. Body muscles and body senses, especially the eyes, build coordination. Repeating certain eye and body movements—catching a ball, for example—builds coordination. Speed is built through brief exercises that demand energy and effort. Short sprints are excellent speed builders.

Conditioning Programs

For hockey, players need to train to maintain their strength and skill levels. Many hockey players participate in a variety of other sports to stay in shape and keep their stamina level high in the off-season. They might follow a program of jogging, running, and working out in a gym. Year-round conditioning is advocated by some coaches, who prepare their athletes by dividing the year into phases or periods, with different goals and objectives for each phase.

Strength

The complete hockey player must be a strong hockey player. A strong body will sustain a player through the rigors of a full season of contact and effort. Here are some basic strength training exercises to keep you in shape:

- **Legs**—You need to be able to skate to play hockey, so you need strong legs. You need to strengthen the muscles in your legs, which include the quadriceps, the hamstrings, the calves, and the hip flexors and extenders.

- **Upper body**—Upper body strength will make your shots harder and faster. Exercises that will help build upper body strength include leg lifts, deep squats with weights, running, push-ups, sit-ups, and jumping jacks.

Skills

The primary way to sharpen your hockey skills, such as stick-handling and shooting, is through practice. Training on dry land, either with a tennis ball or a racquetball, will improve your puck-handling ability. You can even practice this on your driveway. Dry-land stickhandling practice will pay off when you get on the ice.

When off the ice, you can also practice by dribbling the puck on a piece of plastic in your basement while you watch TV. This will help you get the feel of the puck so you don't have to look at it.

Speed

Training yourself to be fast mostly involves your legs. If you do the stretching exercises and you work on speed training, your ice speed should improve.

Reconditioning

A conditioning program is important, but a *reconditioning* program that takes place after an athlete has suffered an injury is crucial. Athletes want to play, but the decision to return to the lineup should be made by the player's parents, family physician, and coach, all working together.

A sprained ankle, for example, might be rehabilitated with easy jogs at first; the player then could build up to running. Ice can be used to reduce swelling, and an elastic bandage may be worn.

Everyone involved should be patient and not allow the player to return to play unless the injury is no longer a problem. Semi-recovered players hurt themselves as much as their team.

8

Safety and First Aid

Hockey safety cannot be overemphasized. No one ever wants to see a player get hurt. Many hockey injuries can be avoided through a preseason medical examination, correct flexibility training, and the proper physical conditioning. Since all athletes do get bumps and bruises, and occasionally more serious injuries, there are a few precautions to keep in mind at games and practices.

Here are some precautions to take when you play or practice hockey:

- Wear the right clothes for practice sessions. Never play without your headgear, mouth gear, or padding.

- Leave any jewelry in your locker or a duffel bag. That includes watches, rings, earrings, etc. This applies to both boys and girls.

- Know where the puck is at all times, to prevent accidental collisions with other players and to avoid getting hit by the puck.

- Stow equipment in one area off the ice.

- Go through a warmup session and do stretching exercises before the actual practice begins. This prevents muscle strains and aches and pains.

• Skip a practice if you are not feeling well. Recovery will be quicker than if you had practiced or competed while under the weather.

• Drink plenty of water. Dehydration can occur quickly. Don't wait until you are thirsty to get a drink. Some coaches recommend sports drinks and think they are useful, but water is just as good, if not better.

• Make sure to keep your stick down so you will not hurt other players.

Coaches may find the following guidelines helpful:

• Always remain calm. Don't panic or appear flustered. Others around you will take their behavior cues from you.

• Don't try to be a doctor. When in doubt about the severity of an injury, send the player to the family physician, or let the on-site doctor, nurse, or health care professional make the decision.

• Never move a player who has a serious injury. Don't try to make the player more comfortable by moving the skater off the ice or into the locker room. This can make a serious injury worse. Be safe, not sorry, and call in the designated professionals if you have doubts about an injury. Under no circumstances should an unconscious hockey player be moved. Stay with the seriously injured player until a professional arrives.

The First Aid Kit

Injuries go hand-in-hand with sports. It's wise to know what to do to handle the inevitable bumps, bruises, scrapes, or more serious injuries. Having a well-stocked first aid kit is recommended. It should include:

• Adhesive tape in different sizes

• Adhesive bandages in different shapes and sizes

• Ammonia caps for dizziness

- Antiseptic solution for minor scrapes

- Antiseptic soap for washing a wound area

- Aspirin, or its equivalent, for simple headaches (Remember: for youth teams, no medication should be given without written permission from a doctor or guardian, signed and dated, authorizing the disbursement of aspirin or other medication)

- Blanket to cover an injured player, since warmth reduces the chance of shock

- Cold packs

- Elastic wraps of various sizes

- Eyewash solution

- Gauze pads

- Hank's solution for a knocked-out tooth (trade name: Save-A-Tooth®)

- Plastic bottle filled with fresh water

- Sterile cotton sheets that can be cut to fit

- Scissors and an eyedropper

- Tweezers

- Tissues and premoistened towelettes

- Disposable towels

Remember that Occupational Safety and Health Administration (OSHA) regulations must be followed when disposing of any items that have blood contamination.

It is a good idea to have a list of emergency telephone numbers taped inside the first aid kit; in a real emergency, however, dial 911. Be sure to keep some spare change inside the first aid kit for use with a pay telephone. At large tournaments it is wise to have a physician, nurse, or other trained health care professional on hand to take care of serious injuries, should they occur. Never assume that precautions have been taken. Check in advance to be sure. Always be prepared. Prior planning prevents problems.

Treatment

Scrapes and Burns

Wash scrapes and burns with an antiseptic cleaning solution and cover with sterile gauze. This is usually all that is needed to promote quick healing of these common injuries.

Small Cuts

Apply pressure to small cuts to slow bleeding. Then wash the area with an antiseptic solution, cover with sterile gauze taped in place, and apply pressure. Of course, any deep cut or large gash may need stitches, so the hockey player should see a doctor as soon as possible.

Blisters

Blisters are fairly common problems for hockey players. Properly fitting skates can go a long way toward preventing these annoying, painful injuries. Any blisters that do occur should be kept clean and covered with a bandage, especially if the blister breaks. Over-the-counter medications to treat blisters are available, but follow the doctor's or coach's suggestions.

Communicable Diseases

Communicable diseases such as boils, athlete's foot, ringworm, and cold sores are common afflictions among hockey players. Mouth sores may be treated with over-the-counter medications, but check with your coach or doctor before using any of these. The best medicine is prevention. Avoid using other players' equipment, and make sure to keep your own equipment clean.

Muscle Pulls, Sprains, and Bruises

Rest, ice, compression, and elevation (**RICE**) are the steps needed to handle these injuries and are about all you should do in the way of treatment. RICE reduces the swelling of most injuries and helps speed recovery.

After a hockey player has been injured, the coach should have the player stop and rest, apply ice, compress the injured area with an elastic bandage, and elevate the injured arm, leg, knee, or ankle. Ice reduces swelling and pain and should be left on the injured area until it becomes uncomfortable. Remove the ice pack and rest for 15 minutes, then reapply. These are the immediate steps to take until a doctor arrives.

Over the next few days the injury should be treated with two to three 20-minute sessions per day at two-and-one-half-hour intervals. This should provide noticeable improvement. Don't overdo the icing; 20 minutes is long enough. In most cases, after two or three days, or when the swelling has stopped, heat can be applied in the form of warm-water soaks. Fifteen minutes of warm soaking, along with a gradual return to motion, will speed the healing process right along.

Another approach to use after two or three days, if the doctor agrees, is to begin motion, strength, and alternative (**MSA**) exercise. The American Institute for Preventive Medicine recommends:

- **Motion**: Move the injured area and reestablish a range of motion.

- **Strength**: Work to increase the strength of the injured area once any inflammation subsides and your range of motion begins to return.

- **Alternative**: Regularly perform an alternative exercise that does not stress the injury.

Seek the advice of a sports-medicine professional prior to starting a treatment plan. Specifically shaped pads are useful for knee and ankle injuries, and they can be used in combination with ice, compression, and elevation. For a simple bruise, apply an ice pack.

Head, Hand, and Foot Injuries

Blows to the upper part of the head, especially near the eyes, can cause bleeding under the skin and result in a black eye. An ice pack applied to the area will reduce the swelling until a doctor can evaluate the injury.

Normally, the eye can wash out most foreign particles because of its ability to produce tears. If this doesn't work, use an eye-cleaning solution to wash out the irritant. If you get something in your eye, a few simple guidelines to follow are:

• Don't rub your eye or use anything dirty, such as a cloth or a finger, to remove the irritant.

• With clean hands, pull the eyelid forward and down as you look at the floor.

• Flush with eyewash, or use a clean, sterile cloth to remove any particle you see in the eye.

If the foreign object remains, the coach should cover the eye with a clean gauze pad and have the athlete visit a doctor.

Nosebleeds usually don't last very long. A hockey player with a nosebleed should sit quietly and apply a cold pack to the bridge of the nose, while pinching the nostril at its base.

A knocked-out tooth can be successfully replanted if it is stored and transported properly. The tooth should be placed in a transport container containing a solution such as Hank's or Viaspan®, which is available over-the-counter at a drugstore. The coach and all medical personnel at a hockey game should be alert to the importance of how to care for a knocked-out tooth. With immediate and proper attention to storage and transport, an injured hockey player may be able to have a knocked-out tooth successfully replanted.

Jammed and/or broken fingers can be hard to distinguish, so use a cold pack to control swelling and pain. If there is no improvement within the hour, the player should have an X-ray.

To safely move a person with an arm, wrist, or hand injury, follow these steps:

• A finger with a mild swelling can be taped to an adjacent finger.

• An elastic bandage may be gently wrapped around an injured wrist to give the wrist support. Do not wrap heavily, and do not pull the bandage tight.

Serious Injuries

Do *not* move a seriously injured hockey player. Instead, get prompt medical attention or call for emergency aid. If you have to wait for assistance, cover the injured player with a lightweight blanket, since warmth will reduce the risk of shock. A hockey player who has broken a bone must be seen by a doctor.

If the hockey player has a possible broken leg or arm, the best approach is *not* to move the leg or arm in any manner. A cold pack can be used to lessen the discomfort until medical personnel arrive, and the player should be kept warm with a blanket.

A fracture can be recognized by some or all of the following:

• A part of the body is bent or twisted out of its normal shape.
• A bone has pierced the skin.
• Swelling is severe and more than the swelling associated with a typical sprain or bruise.
• The hand or foot becomes extremely cold, which may indicate pinching of a major blood vessel.

Youngsters heal faster than adults, so it is important to get them prompt medical attention when a fracture occurs.

Breathing Problems and Other Health Issues

Getting the wind "knocked out of you" happens to all hockey players sooner or later. Not much can be done to prevent this, and not much can be done to treat this. Your breathing will return to normal faster if you can relax and take easy breaths.

By following the guidelines in this chapter, the extent and severity of injuries can be reduced and treatment minimized, so the player can return to the ice confidently. Knowing what to do is beneficial to the players, coaches, and parents in and out of the sport.

9

Guidelines

For everyone to enjoy a hockey game, good sportsmanship must extend beyond the field of play and include parents and spectators as well as coaches.

Parents

Hockey is meant to be fun for all involved. Parents of developing hockey players need to be supportive and enthusiastic about the sport, and focus on the young athletes' achievements rather than miscues. This attitude will build the confidence a youngster needs to succeed, not just in sports but in many other aspects of life. Parents are the earliest role models for their children; consequently, children carry over into sports the attitudes they learn from their parents.

Parents want their children to excel, to rise to the top, to be winners. Understandably, many parents want to bask in their children's glory. The problem is that hockey is a competitive team sport, and one team will usually finish the game with fewer goals than the other. Parents need to be prepared to handle defeat in an adult manner, by praising the effort involved and by avoiding a litany of "What you (or the team or the coach) should have done was. ..." Most youngsters are usually well aware of their skills and limitations, and they don't need to be told or made to feel somehow deficient when their team loses. Parents should recognize the achievement of the winning team and never criticize the referees or coaches. Coaches and referees are usually volunteers. Often they are parents who have children involved in the sport. They have the same emotions as parents—in fact, their feelings may be even more intense, since they are more directly involved. They have to be objective, treat all players with the same respect and regard, and follow the rules. Noncoaching parents have similar obligations.

Children benefit from participating in hockey, and the confidence they gain carries over to other parts of life: working with others, developing self-discipline, learning good health habits, and acquiring self-esteem. Psychological as well as physical benefits are involved, as athletes develop a positive channel for their youthful energy. A recent finding of the President's Council on Physical Fitness and Sports stated that athletics promote health in adulthood, and reduce the incidence of stress and depression. Furthermore, athletes stay in school and seem more motivated to continue their education by attending college.

Young girls, especially, need encouragement to participate in sports such as hockey, which for years have been promoted as "male only" activities. Stereotypes abound about athletics not being "feminine," and many young women tune out sports because of the negative stereotypes. Parents can help daughters to overcome these stereotypes by demonstrating an interest in sports, especially in any sports that interest their children. Encourage, but don't push.

Before a child becomes involved in a particular sport, parents should decide whether that child is physically and psychologically ready for a competitive sport. A preseason physical from the family physician is the first step in determining whether a youngster is healthy and would benefit from participation. The child is still growing, so parents, the coach, and assistants should recognize and make allowances for this. (Ideally, children should play with other children of nearly the same size, not necessarily the same age.)

Don't hesitate to inquire about the coach's qualifications and experience. Training in all phases of the game should be given by someone who is knowledgeable and trained in the proper methods. Incorrect training can cause nagging injuries that decrease the enjoyment of the game for everyone.

Enthusiasm for the sport may drop off after a few practices or games. A parent should try to be fairly certain of the child's commitment and ability to work and play easily with other youngsters before signing up for hockey. Recent studies of young athletes indicate that the quality of their play improves when parents attend games. In addition to a youngster's commitment, his parents should also make one.

Fans

Prior to attending a hockey game, learn the basics of the sport, and your enjoyment will increase appreciably. Observing some common courtesies will also ensure that you'll be welcome at every game. Always remain seated and calm, keep your comments about the players and referees positive, and be respectful to others seated around you.

Volunteers

Being a volunteer requires extra time and a desire to a make a difference in the lives of young people. Volunteering is a rewarding experience, and hockey provides numerous opportunities for people to volunteer both time and energy. Young people look to adults for guidance, support, and direction. Setting a positive example by giving of your time is a wonderful way to contribute to a young person's view of adults.

There are many ways to help a local youth hockey team, whether as a coach or leader, referee, or fan. When the community is sponsoring a tournament, there are a variety of ways to help.

- Staff the on-site registration table.
- Be the scorekeeper, announcer, or timekeeper.
- Prepare forms, information sheets, and maps.
- Act as the tournament coordinator.
- Work on the cleanup committee.
- Help coordinate other volunteers.
- Be the equipment manager.
- Be the treasurer.
- Be the photographer.
- Videotape practices for use by all players and coaches.
- Arrange transportation to and from both home and away games.

Teams and Players

Learning to be a member of a team teaches many of the most important skills necessary for success and enjoyment throughout one's life. Working together, within a prescribed set of rules, toward a worthwhile goal rewards everyone involved with a sense of accomplishment and pride in the united effort. Regardless of the outcome, everyone who participates in a positive spirit is a winner. Working within a group often requires putting aside individual goals for the sake of the team, an important lesson in selflessness and compromise. Helpfulness and dependability are required attributes of every team member, and are also vital life skills.

There are a number of things a player can do for the good of the team:

- Support everyone on the team equally.

- Offer encouragement at all times, no matter what the score might be.

- Learn how to win—and lose—graciously.

- Always stay positive and complimentary regarding others' skills.

- Let coaches correct errors—that's their role.

- Play within the rules at all times; don't show off.

- Attend every practice, meeting, and game you can. Be on time.

- Don't dwell on mistakes—yours or anyone else's.

- Never taunt an opponent or referee.

- Set a good example by staying healthy and ready to play at a high level.

As a hockey player, keep the sport in perspective and make sure it fits properly into your overall life. Stay healthy and fit, and get plenty of sleep. Many schools and teams require a certain level of academic achievement in order to participate in sports and other extracurricular activities. Therefore, school attendance and performance must always come first when prioritizing your life. Playing hockey should be an enjoyable and rewarding experience—keep it in proper perspective.

Remember that your actions reflect not only on yourself but also on your community and on the sport. Players should act in such a way as to be a credit to their community and to the sport. All sports evolve over time, based on the actions of those involved. Be a player who advances hockey through a strong, positive attitude, and you will enjoy every ounce of energy you put into it, regardless of the outcome of any particular game.

10

Glossary

Assist A point credited in the scoring record to the offensive player or players involved in the play immediately preceding a goal. No more than two assists may be awarded for each goal scored.

Backchecking The action of the forwards as they skate back into their defensive zone to break up the opposing team's attack.

Body check Use of the body to impede an opponent who has possession of the puck, in order to break up or disrupt an offensive play.

Breakaway A scoring opportunity that occurs when there are no defending players between the puck carrier and the opposing goaltender.

Breakout Movement of the attacking team out of its defensive zone and up ice.

Changing on the fly Substitution of players without a stoppage in play.

Clearing the puck Shooting the puck out of the defensive zone or away from the front of the goal.

Delayed penalty 1. A penalty that occurs when a team has only the minimum of four players on the ice because two players are in the penalty box. If the same team receives a third penalty, it doesn't take full effect until one of the preceding penalties has terminated. 2. A penalty not called by the referee until the offending team has touched the puck.

Delayed whistle After a violation, a delay by the referee in stopping play while the non-offending team remains in possession of the puck. The moment the offending team touches the puck, play will be stopped.

Face-off The method by which play is initiated or restarted. The official drops the puck between two opposing players, who use their sticks to try to complete a pass to a teammate or a shot on goal.

Forechecking Pressuring the opposing team members when they control the puck in their half of the neutral zone or in their defensive zone.

Goal crease The area marked off in front of the goal. An offensive player may not enter the goal crease unless the puck is already inside this area and not under the control of the goalie.

Goal judge An off-ice official who sits behind the goal, outside the boards, and determines whether the puck has entered the goal. Should there be a difference of opinion, the referee makes the final decision.

Hat trick	The scoring of three or more goals by the same player in a single game.
Ice Resurfacer	A machine used to resurface the ice between periods.
Icing	An infraction that occurs when, while both teams have an equal number of players on the ice, a player on one team shoots the puck from behind the center red line across the opponent's goal line (unless the puck goes into the goal). In some leagues, such as the NHL and Major Junior Hockey, the puck must first be touched by a player from the defensive team before icing is called
Minor officials	Often referred to as "off-ice officials." These include the goal judges, game timer, penalty timer, and official scorer.
Offside pass	A pass from a team's defensive zone to a player of the same team who is beyond the center red line.
Offsides penalty	An infraction that occurs when an offensive player precedes the puck across the blue line and into the offensive zone. A face-off is then held in the neutral zone.
Poke check	A check made by using the blade of the stick to knock the puck away from an opponent.
Power play	Attacking maneuver used by a team that has a numerical advantage in players due to a penalty or penalties.
Referee's crease	A restricted area marked by a red semicircle, in front of the timer's table. Players are

prohibited from entering this area while the referee is reporting a penalty.

Screen An offensive maneuver in which attacking players position themselves to block or shield the opposing goaltender's view of the puck.

Shorthanded A term that describes the situation of a team which, because of penalties, is playing with one or two fewer players on the ice than the opposing team.

Slap shot A shot taken using a sweeping motion with an accentuated back swing (similar to a drive in golf).

Slot An unmarked area in front of the goal, approximately 10–15 feet in diameter.

Wrist shot A shot taken with the puck directly against the blade of the stick.

11

Olympic and Ice Hockey Organizations

The organization of, and participation in, the Olympic Games requires the cooperation of a number of independent organizations.

The International Olympic Committee (IOC)

The IOC is responsible for determining where the Games will be held. It is also the obligation of its membership to uphold the principles of the Olympic Ideal and Philosophy beyond any personal, religious, national, or political interest. The IOC is responsible for sustaining the Olympic Movement.

The members of the IOC are individuals who act as the IOC's representatives in their respective countries, not as delegates of their countries within the IOC. The members meet once a year at the IOC Session. They retire at the end of the calendar year in which they turn 70 years old, unless they were elected before the opening of the 110th Session (December 11, 1999). In that case, they must retire at the age of 80. Members elected before 1966 are members for life. The IOC chooses and elects its members from among such persons as its nominations committee considers qualified. There are currently 113 members and 19 honorary members.

The International Olympic Committee's address is:
Chateau de Vidy
Case Postale 356
1007 Lausanne, Switzerland
phone: (+41) 21 621 61 11
fax: (+41) 21 621 6216
Internet: http://www.olympic.org

The National Olympic Committees

Olympic Committees have been created with the design and objectives of the IOC to prepare national teams to participate in the Olympic Games. Among the tasks of these committees is to promote the Olympic Movement and its principles at the national level.

The national committees work closely with the IOC in all aspects related to the Games. They are also responsible for applying the rules concerning eligibility of athletes for the Games. Today there are more than 150 national committees throughout the world.

The U.S. Olympic Committee's address is:
One Olympic Plaza
Colorado Springs, CO 80909-5760
phone: (719) 632-5551
fax: (719) 578-4654
Internet: http://www.usolympicteam.com

International Ice Hockey Federation (IIHF)

Parkring 11
8002 Zurich, Switzerland
phone: 41-1-289-8600
fax: 41-1-289-8622
Internet: http://www.iihf.com

USA Hockey, Inc.

1775 Bob Johnson Drive
Colorado Springs, CO 80906-4090
phone: (719) 576-8724   fax: (719) 538-1160

E-mail: usah@usahockey.org
Internet: http://www.usahockey.com

USA Hockey, Inc., is the national governing body for the sport of hockey in the United States. It is the official representative to the U.S. Olympic Committee (USOC) and the International Ice Hockey Federation (IIHF). In this role, USA Hockey is responsible for organizing and training men's and women's teams for international tournaments that include the IIHF World Championships and the Olympic Winter Games. USA Hockey also coordinates activities with other national hockey federations around the world and, closer to home, works with the National Hockey League (NHL) and the National Collegiate Athletic Association (NCAA) on matters of mutual interest.

With a membership of more than 580,000 ice and inline hockey players, coaches, officials, and volunteers, USA Hockey's primary emphasis is on the support and development of grassroots hockey programs. The organization annually conducts regional and national championship tournaments in various age classifications; sponsors regional and national player identification and development camps; studies and makes recommendations for protective equipment; and distributes Hat Trick, Playmaker, and Zero Club awards. USA Hockey also conducts clinics and produces training manuals and videos through the Coaching Education Program and the Officiating Education Program. USA Hockey publications include *American Hockey Magazine* and a "Parent's Introduction to Youth Hockey" brochure that provides tips on buying equipment, rules of the game, and the role of parents in youth sports.

In December 1994, USA Hockey introduced its official inline hockey program, USA Hockey InLine. Membership packages include standardized playing rules, competitive playing opportunities at the regional and national levels, and a variety of educational programs for players, coaches, and officials.